This Book Belongs

My name is _____

I am _____ years old.

My parent(s) names are _____

_____

My address is _____

_____

My telephone number is _____

Get Ready for Kindergarten

270 INTERACTIVE ACTIVITIES AND 2,158 ILLUSTRATIONS THAT MAKE LEARNING FUN!

Jane Carole

BLACK DOG
& LEVENTHAL
PUBLISHERS
NEW YORK

ISBN-13: 978-1-60376-133-8
Library of Congress Cataloging-in-Publication Data on file
at the offices of Black Dog & Leventhal Publishers, Inc.

Original Italian text by P. Holeinone, A. Magoo, E. Dami, M. Drago, A. Sirena
Illustrations by Matt Wolf and Tony Wolf
Book design by Mark Weinberg

Special thanks to LeeAnn Bortolussi, Deborah Brody, Helen Capone, Andrea Dami,
Kylie Foxx, Mary Ann Laborda, J.P. Leventhal, Laura Ross, and True Sims.

Manufactured in China

Published by
Black Dog & Leventhal Publishers, Inc.
151 West 19th Street
New York, New York 10011

Contents

A Note to Parents

Get Ready for Kindergarten is an indispensable educational companion for your pre-kindergarten child. It is chock full of fun, interesting, curriculum-based activities—such as those focusing on the alphabet, numbers, colors, shapes, math readiness, nature, and more—that will introduce your child to new concepts while reinforcing what he or she already knows. In addition, there are plenty of fun word games, mazes, coloring activities, and crafts that are designed to entertain and amuse your child while boosting his or her basic skills.

In the back of the book you will find a Suggested Reading List. We recommend setting aside some time each day to read with your child. The more your child reads,

the faster he or she will acquire other skills. We also suggest that you have your child complete a portion of the book each day. You and your child can sit down and discuss what the goals for each day will be, and perhaps even choose a reward to be given upon completion of the whole book—such as a trip to the park, a special play date, or something else that seems appropriate to you. While you want to help your child set educational goals, be sure to offer lots of encouragement along the way. These activities are not meant as a test. By making them fun and rewarding, you will help your child look forward to completing them, and he or she will be especially eager to tackle the educational challenges ahead!

Hey Kids!
Remember to have
a pencil and
some crayons
handy when
playing with your
Get Ready book!

The

Alphabet

The Alphabet

Aa Bb Cc Dd

Ee Ff Gg Hh

Ii Jj Kk Ll Mm

Nn Oo Pp Qq

Rr Ss Tt Uu Vv

Ww Xx Yy Zz

The Alphabet Game

Point to each letter of the alphabet and say it out loud.
What can you think of that begins with that letter?
Is there anything you can spot nearby that begins with that letter?
Name as many things as you can.

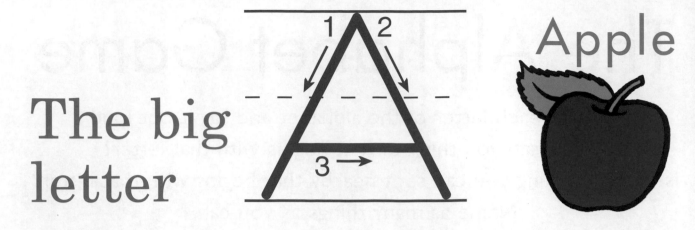

The big letter

Apple

This is the big letter A. Use your finger to trace it.
Now practice writing the big letter A by following the arrows.

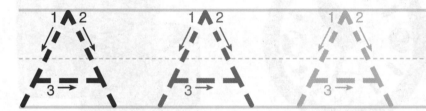

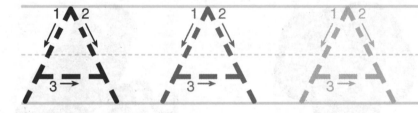

Astronaut

The little letter 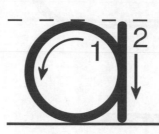 airplane

This is the little letter a. Use your finger to trace it.
Now practice writing the little letter a by following the arrows.

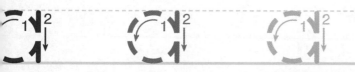

Practice writing both the big letter A and little letter a on a separate piece of paper.

The big letter

Banana

This is the big letter B. Use your finger to trace it.
Now practice writing the big letter B by following the arrows.

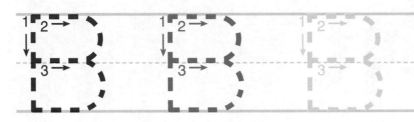

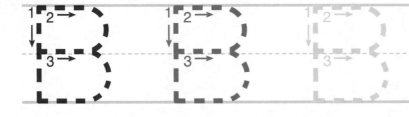

Book

The little letter

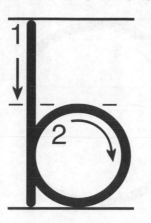

bicycle

This is the little letter b. Use your finger to trace it.
Now practice writing the little letter b by following the arrows.

Practice writing both the big letter B and little letter b on a separate piece of paper.

The big letter C

This is the big letter C. Use your finger to trace it.
Now practice writing the big letter C by following the arrows.

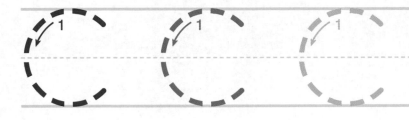

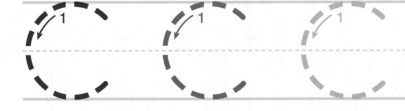

Clown

The little letter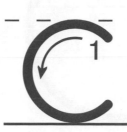

camera

This is the little letter C. Use your finger to trace it.
Now practice writing the little letter C by following the arrows.

Practice writing both the big letter C and little letter C on a separate piece of paper.

The big letter

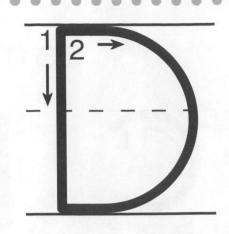

Doll

This is the big letter D. Use your finger to trace it.
Now practice writing the big letter D by following the arrows.

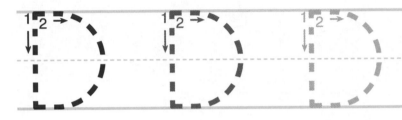

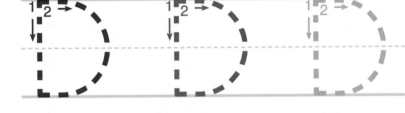

Doctor

The little letter

drum

This is the little letter d. Use your finger to trace it.
Now practice writing the little letter d by following the arrows.

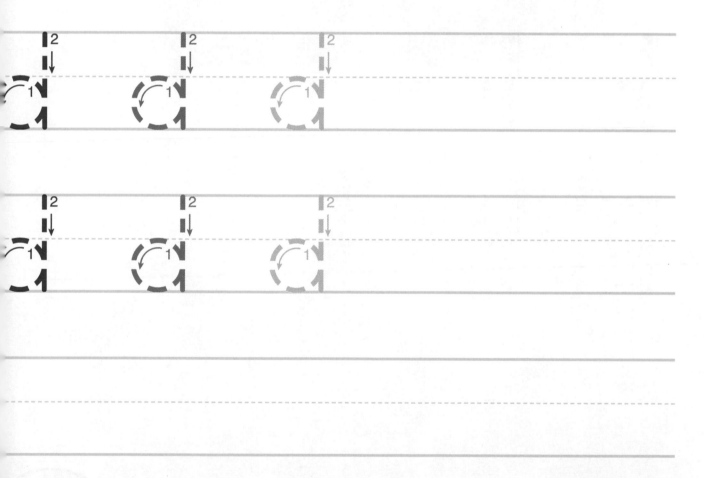

Practice writing both the big letter D and little letter d on a separate piece of paper.

The big letter

Eggs

This is the big letter E. Use your finger to trace it.
Now practice writing the big letter E by following the arrows.

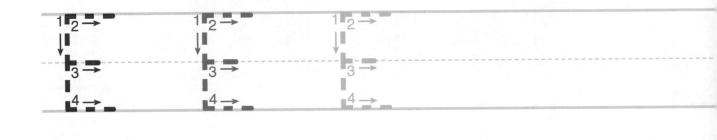

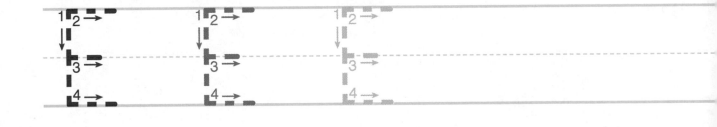

Elephant

The little letter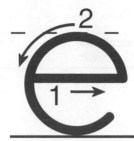

earmuffs

This is the little letter e. Use your finger to trace it.
Now practice writing the little letter e by following the arrows.

Practice writing both the big letter E and little letter e on a separate piece of paper.

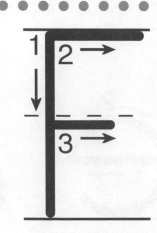

The big letter

Fire Truck

This is the big letter F. Use your finger to trace it.
Now practice writing the big letter F by following the arrows.

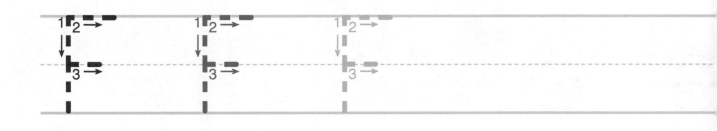

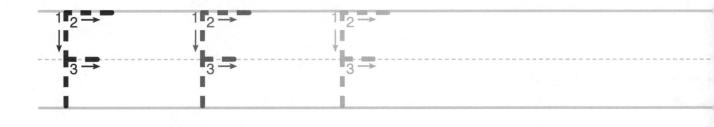

Flower

The little letter

frog

This is the little letter f. Use your finger to trace it.
Now practice writing the little letter f by following the arrows.

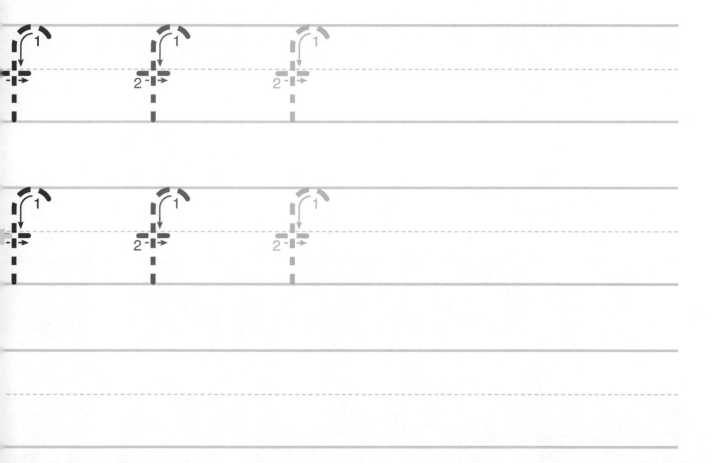

Practice writing both the big letter F and little letter f on a separate piece of paper.

The big letter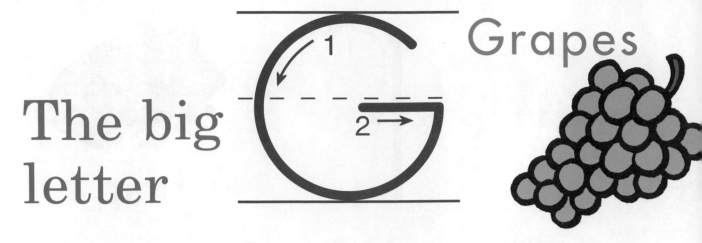

Grapes

This is the big letter G. Use your finger to trace it.
Now practice writing the big letter G by following the arrows.

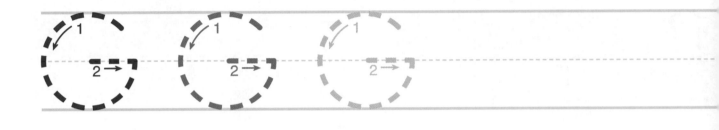

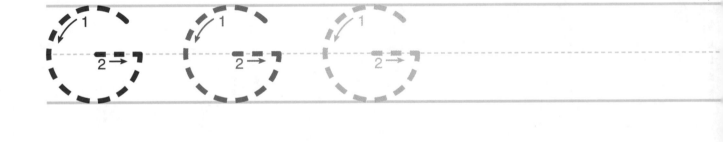

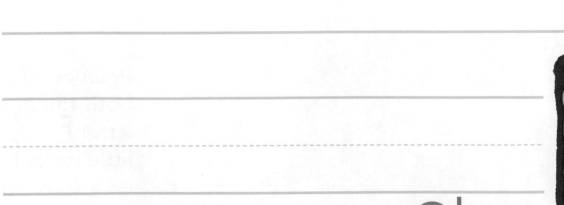

Glass

The little letter 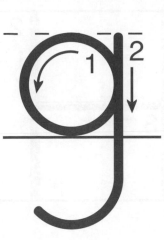 gorilla

This is the little letter g. Use your finger to trace it.
Now practice writing the little letter g by following the arrows.

Practice writing both the big letter G and little letter g on a separate piece of paper.

The big letter

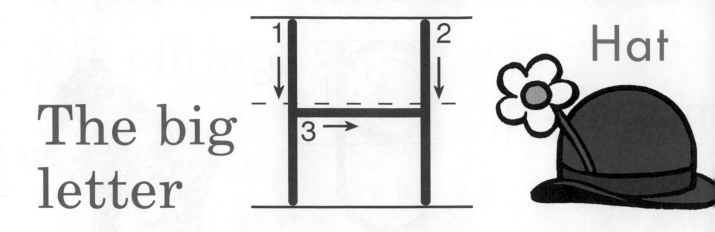

Hat

This is the big letter H. Use your finger to trace it.
Now practice writing the big letter H by following the arrows.

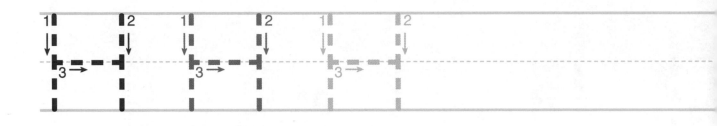

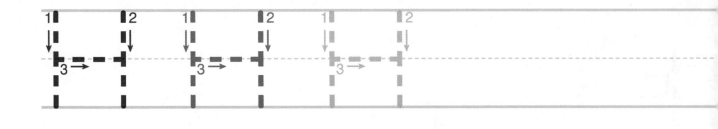

Hippopotamu

The little letter

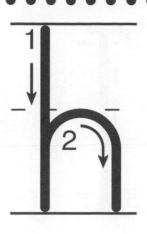

helicopter

This is the little letter h. Use your finger to trace it.
Now practice writing the little letter h by following the arrows.

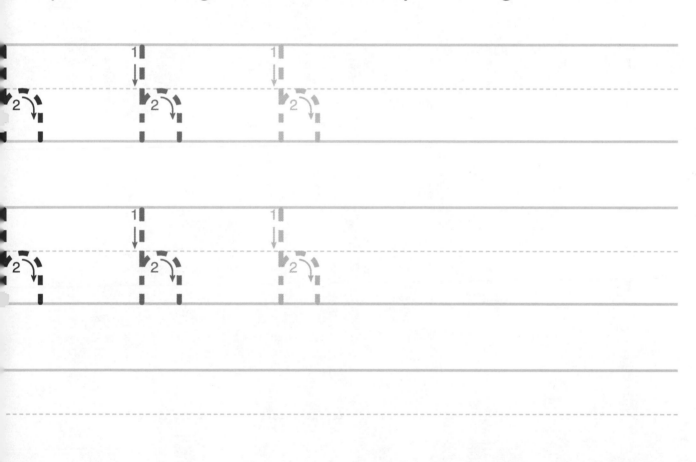

Practice writing
both the big
letter H and
little letter h
on a separate
piece of paper.

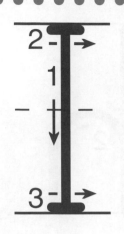

The big letter

Igloo

This is the big letter I. Use your finger to trace it.
Now practice writing the big letter I by following the arrows.

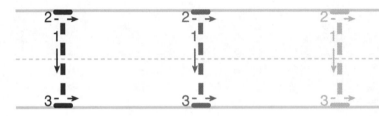

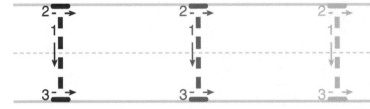

Ice cream

The little letter i

iron

This is the little letter i. Use your finger to trace it.
Now practice writing the little letter i by following the arrows.

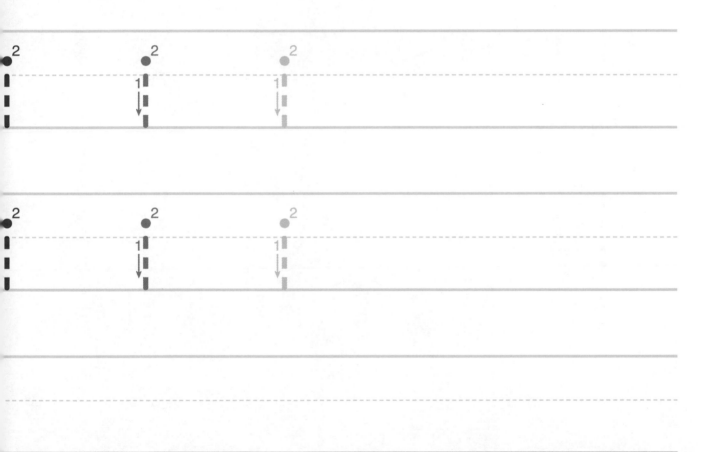

Practice writing
both the big
letter I and
little letter i
on a separate
piece of paper.

The big letter

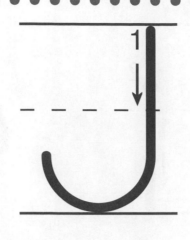

Jeep

This is the big letter J. Use your finger to trace it.
Now practice writing the big letter J by following the arrows.

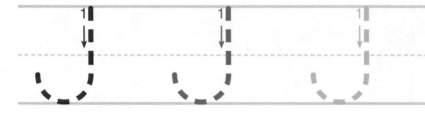

Judge

The little letter

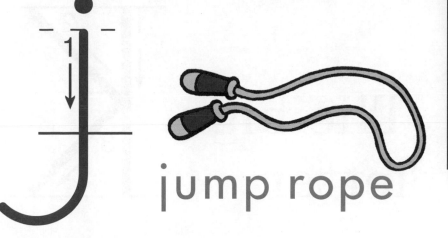

j

jump rope

This is the little letter j. Use your finger to trace it.
Now practice writing the little letter j by following the arrows.

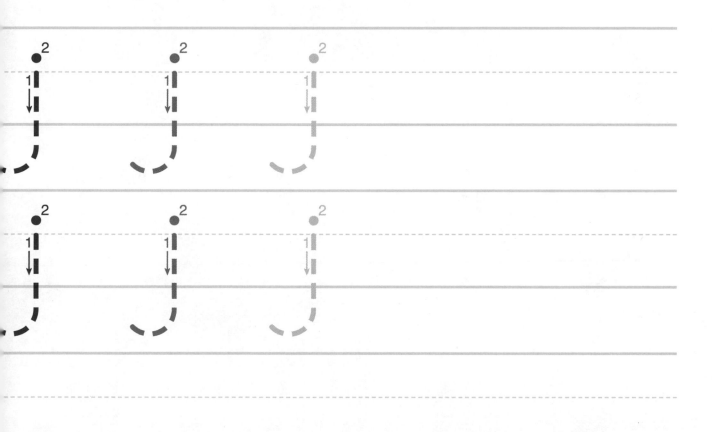

Practice writing both the big letter J and little letter j on a separate piece of paper.

The big letter

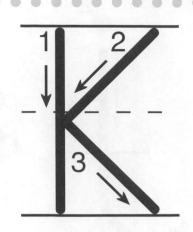

Kite

This is the big letter K. Use your finger to trace it.
Now practice writing the big letter K by following the arrows.

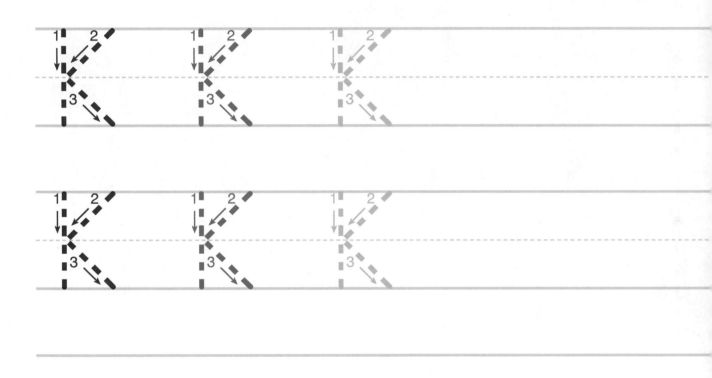

Koala

The little letter

key

This is the little letter k. Use your finger to trace it.
Now practice writing the little letter k by following the arrows.

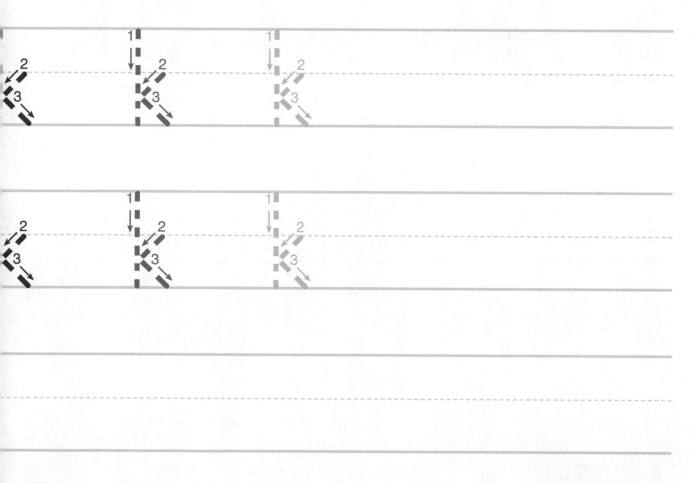

Practice writing both the big letter K and little letter k on a separate piece of paper.

The big letter

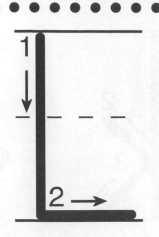

This is the big letter L. Use your finger to trace it.
Now practice writing the big letter L by following the arrows.

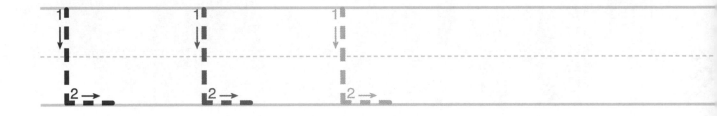

Ladybug

The little letter
etter

lamp

his is the little letter l. Use your finger to trace it.
low practice writing the little letter l by following the arrows.

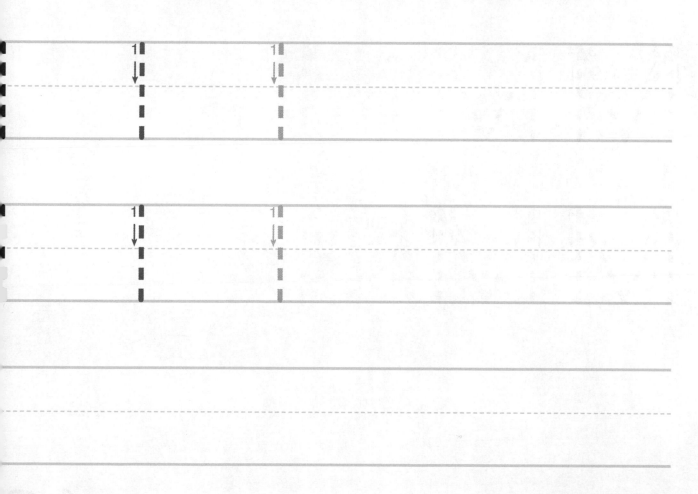

Practice writing both the big letter L and little letter l on a separate piece of paper.

The big letter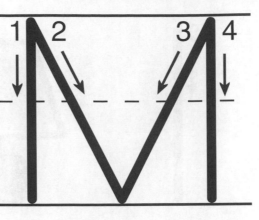

Mouse

This is the big letter M. Use your finger to trace it.
Now practice writing the big letter M by following the arrows.

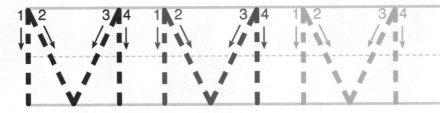

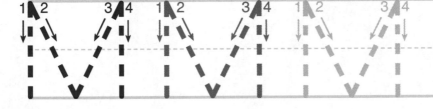

Magicia

mushroom

The little letter

This is the little letter m. Use your finger to trace it.
Now practice writing the little letter m by following the arrows.

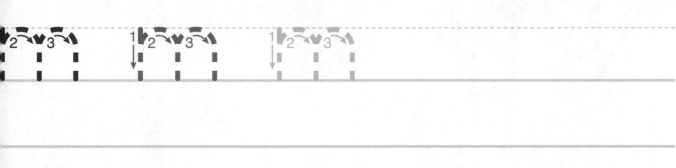

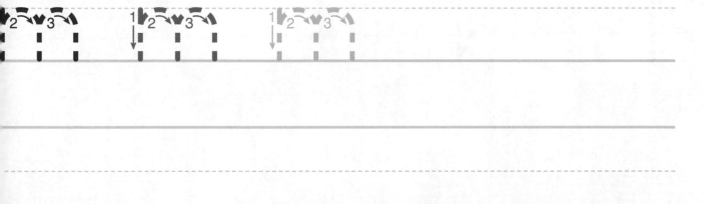

Practice writing both the big letter M and little letter m on a separate piece of paper.

The big letter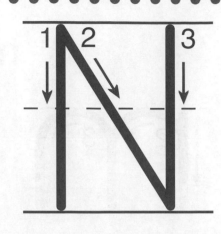

Nest

This is the big letter N. Use your finger to trace it.
Now practice writing the big letter N by following the arrows.

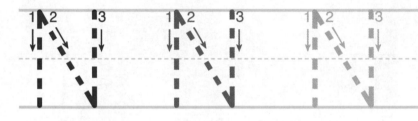

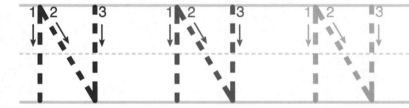

Needle

The little letter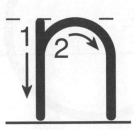

nut

This is the little letter n. Use your finger to trace it.
Now practice writing the little letter n by following the arrows.

Practice writing both the big letter N and little letter n on a separate piece of paper.

The big letter

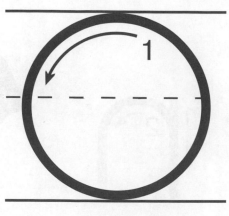

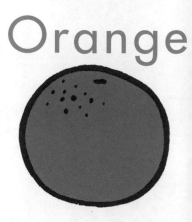

This is the big letter O. Use your finger to trace it.
Now practice writing the big letter O by following the arrows.

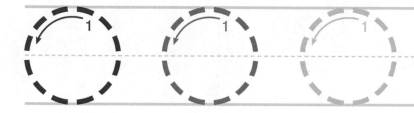

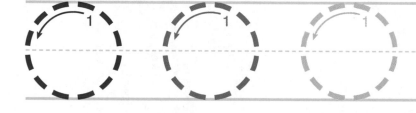

Owl

The little letter  octopus

This is the little letter O. Use your finger to trace it.
Now practice writing the little letter O by following the arrows.

Practice writing both the big letter O and little letter o on a separate piece of paper.

The big letter

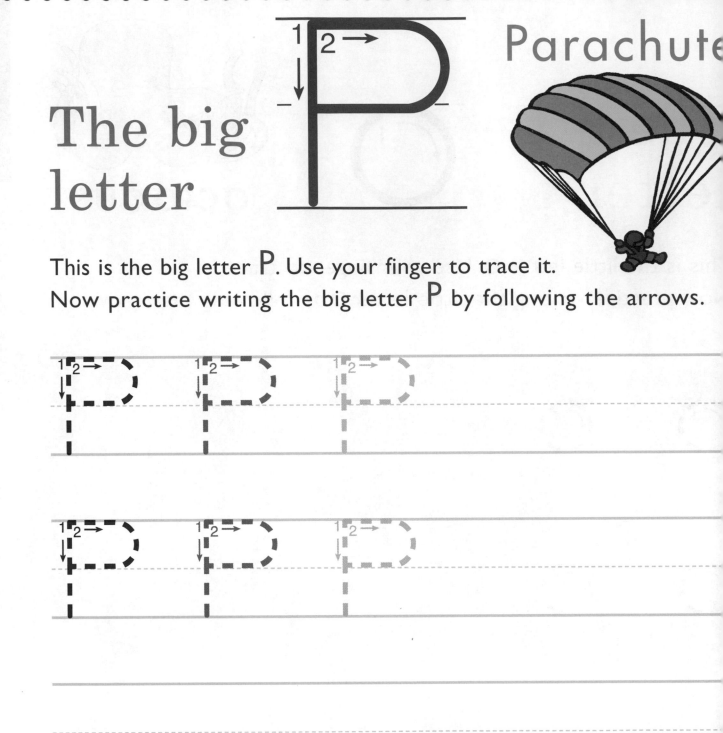

Parachute

This is the big letter P. Use your finger to trace it.
Now practice writing the big letter P by following the arrows.

Penguin

The little letter

pumpkin

This is the little letter p. Use your finger to trace it.
Now practice writing the little letter p by following the arrows.

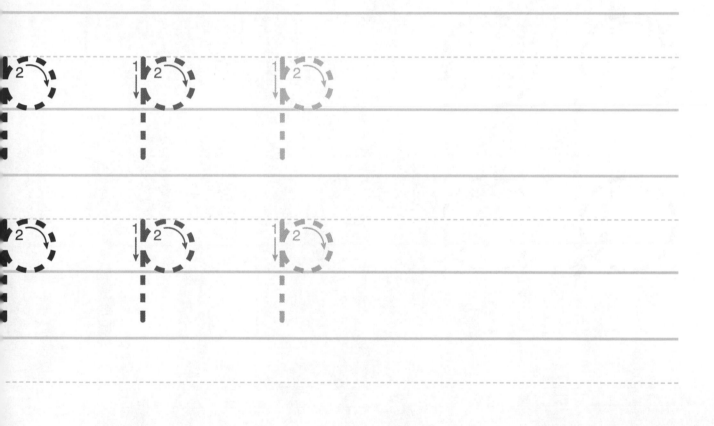

Practice writing both the big letter P and little letter p on a separate piece of paper.

The big letter

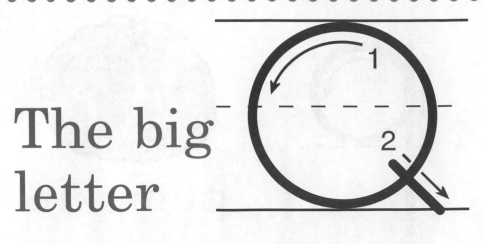

This is the big letter Q. Use your finger to trace it.
Now practice writing the big letter Q by following the arrows.

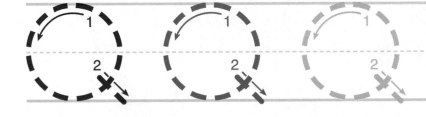

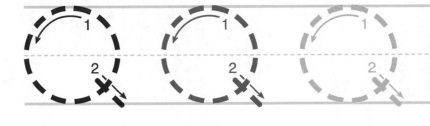

Quilt

The little letter

quail

This is the little letter q. Use your finger to trace it.
Now practice writing the little letter q by following the arrows.

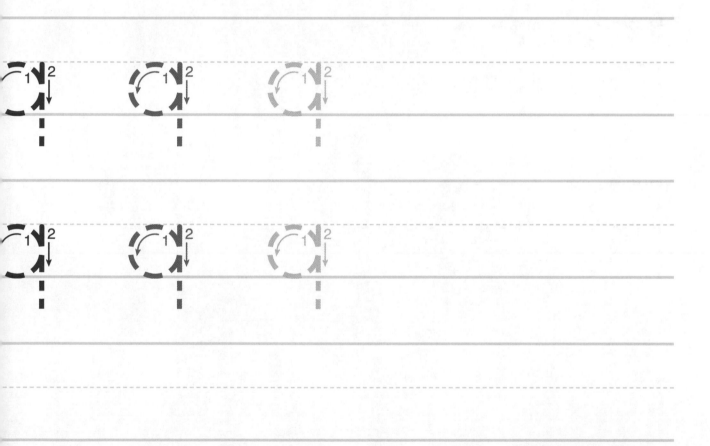

Practice writing
both the big
letter Q and
little letter q
on a separate
piece of paper.

The big letter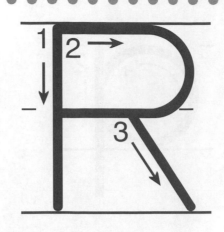

Rose

This is the big letter R. Use your finger to trace it.
Now practice writing the big letter R by following the arrows.

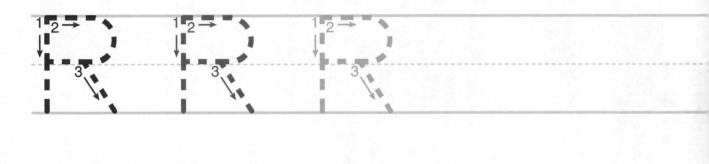

Robot

The little letter

rooster

This is the little letter r. Use your finger to trace it.
Now practice writing the little letter r by following the arrows.

Practice writing
both the big
letter R and
little letter r
on a separate
piece of paper.

The big letter

Strawberry

This is the big letter S. Use your finger to trace it.
Now practice writing the big letter S by following the arrows.

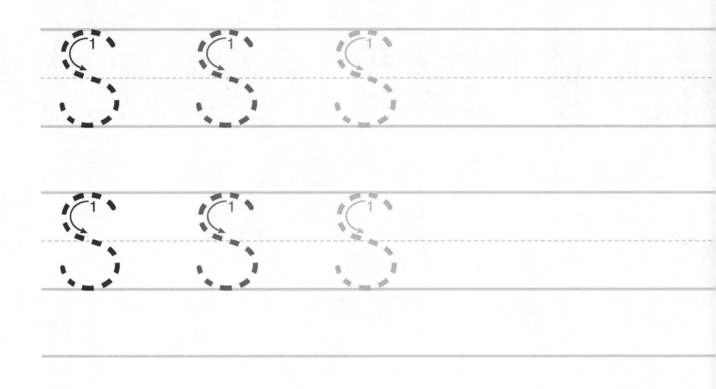

Snail

The little letter S

submarine

This is the little letter S. Use your finger to trace it.
Now practice writing the little letter S by following the arrows.

Practice writing
both the big
letter S and
little letter S
on a separate
piece of paper.

Tracto

The big letter

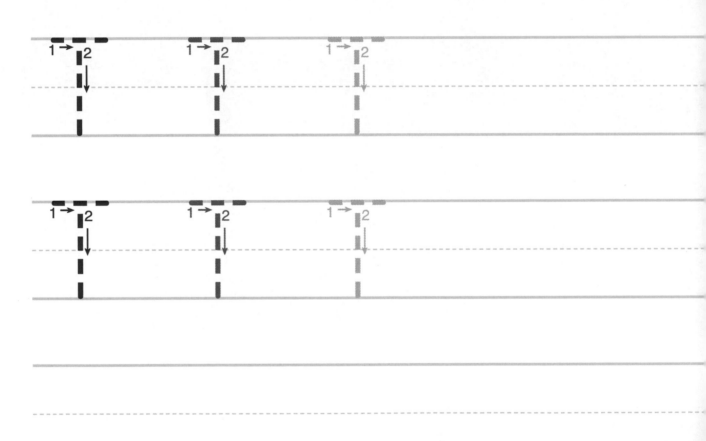

This is the big letter T. Use your finger to trace it.
Now practice writing the big letter T by following the arrows.

Tailor

The little letter

telephone

This is the little letter t. Use your finger to trace it.
Now practice writing the little letter t by following the arrows.

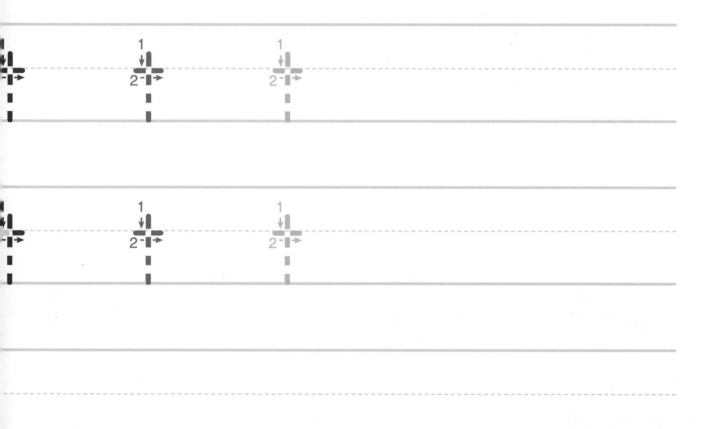

Practice writing
both the big
letter T and
little letter t
on a separate
piece of paper.

The big letter

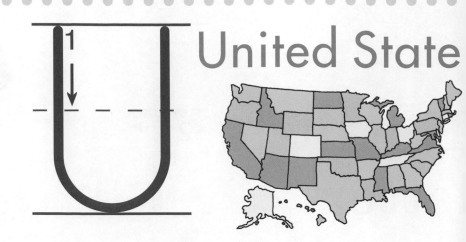

United State

This is the big letter U. Use your finger to trace it.
Now practice writing the big letter U by following the arrows.

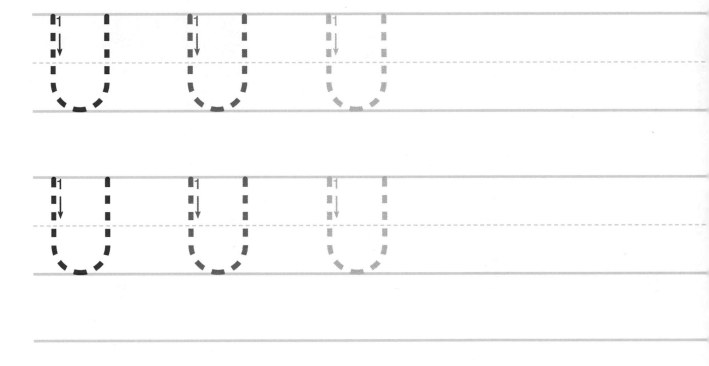

Umbrella

The little letter 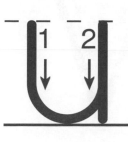 letter

underwear

This is the little letter **U**. Use your finger to trace it.
Now practice writing the little letter **U** by following the arrows.

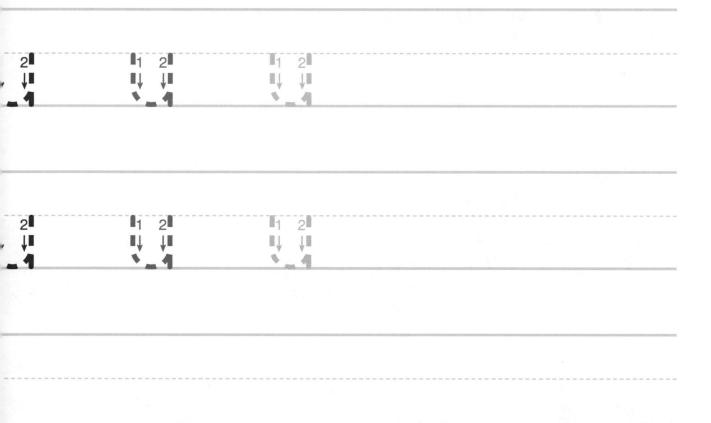

Practice writing both the big letter U and little letter **U** on a separate piece of paper.

The big letter

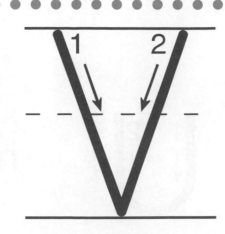

Volcano

This is the big letter V. Use your finger to trace it.
Now practice writing the big letter V by following the arrows.

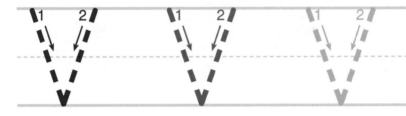

Vacuum

The little letter 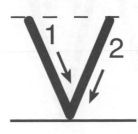  vegetables

This is the little letter V. Use your finger to trace it.
Now practice writing the little letter V by following the arrows.

Practice writing both the big letter V and little letter V on a separate piece of paper.

The big letter

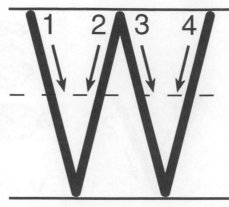

Whale

This is the big letter W. Use your finger to trace it.
Now practice writing the big letter W by following the arrows.

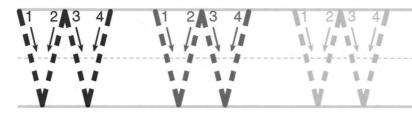

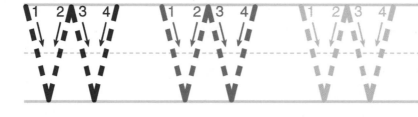

Waiter

watermelon

The little letter

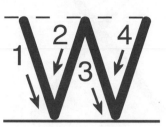

letter

This is the little letter W. Use your finger to trace it.
Now practice writing the little letter W by following the arrows.

Practice writing both the big letter **W** and little letter W on a separate piece of paper.

The big letter X

Xylophone

This is the big letter X. Use your finger to trace it.
Now practice writing the big letter X by following the arrows.

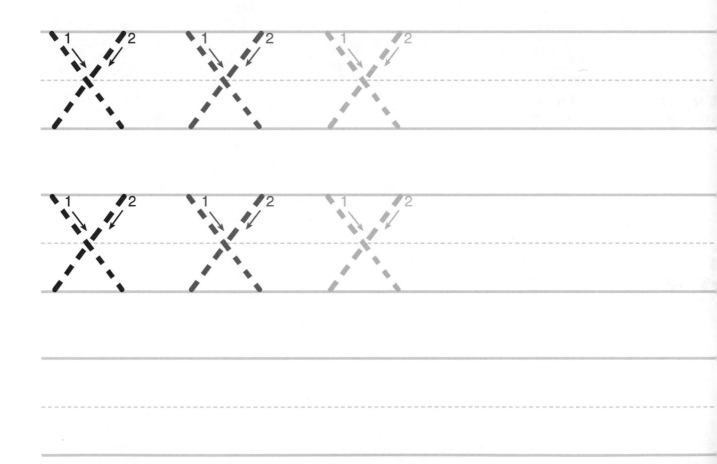

The little letter

x-ray

This is the little letter X. Use your finger to trace it.
Now practice writing the little letter X by following the arrows.

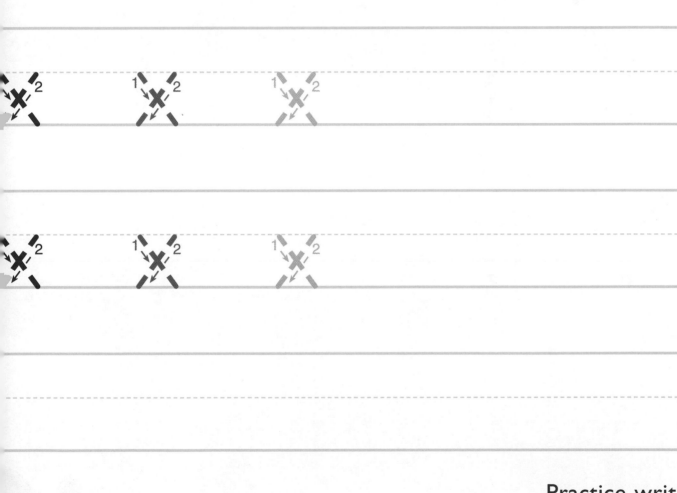

Practice writing both the big letter X and little letter X on a separate piece of paper.

The big letter

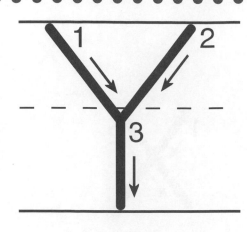

Yogurt

This is the big letter Y. Use your finger to trace it.
Now practice writing the big letter Y by following the arrows.

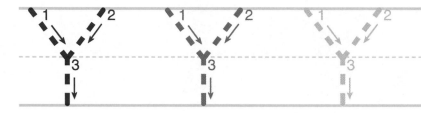

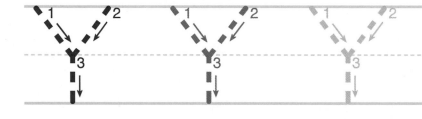

yellowjacke

The little letter

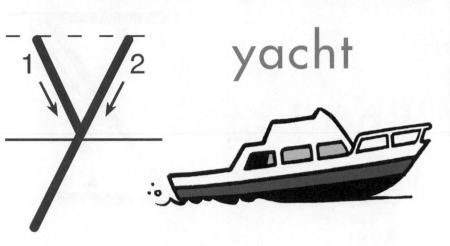

yacht

This is the little letter y. Use your finger to trace it.
Now practice writing the little letter y by following the arrows.

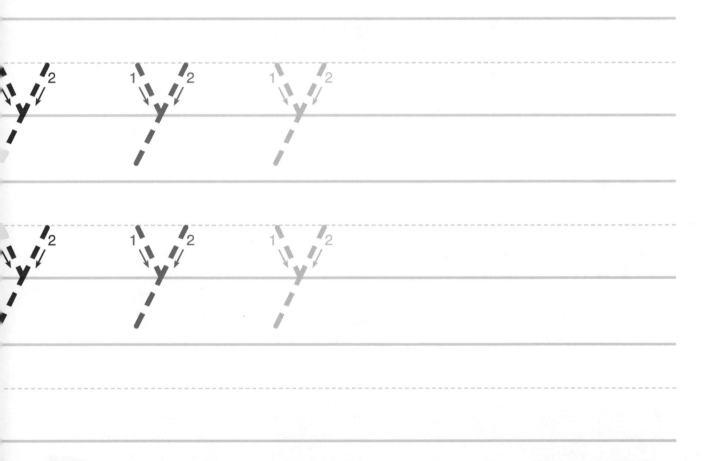

Practice writing both the big letter Y and little letter y on a separate piece of paper.

The big letter

Z

Zebra

This is the big letter Z. Use your finger to trace it.
Now practice writing the big letter Z by following the arrows.

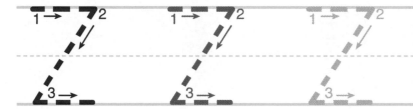

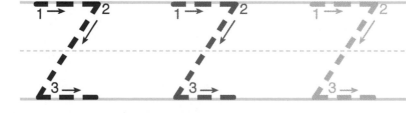

Zucchini

The little letter 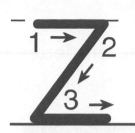 Z zeppelin

This is the little letter Z. Use your finger to trace it.
Now practice writing the little letter Z by following the arrows.

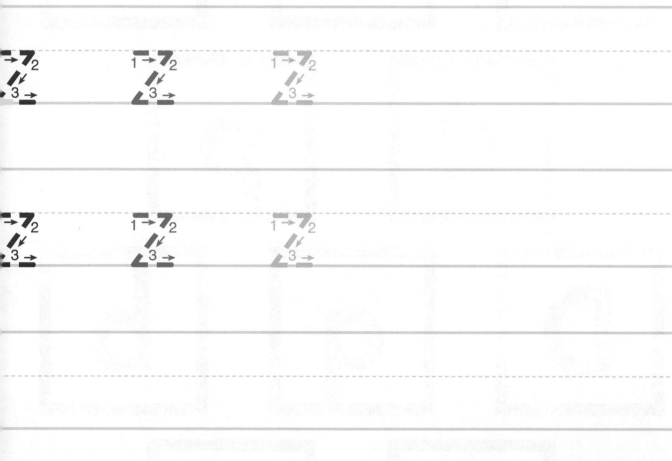

Practice writing both the big letter Z and little letter Z on a separate piece of paper.

The Letter D

Each of these squares has a different letter inside it. Color only the squares where you find either the big letter **D** or little letter **d**.

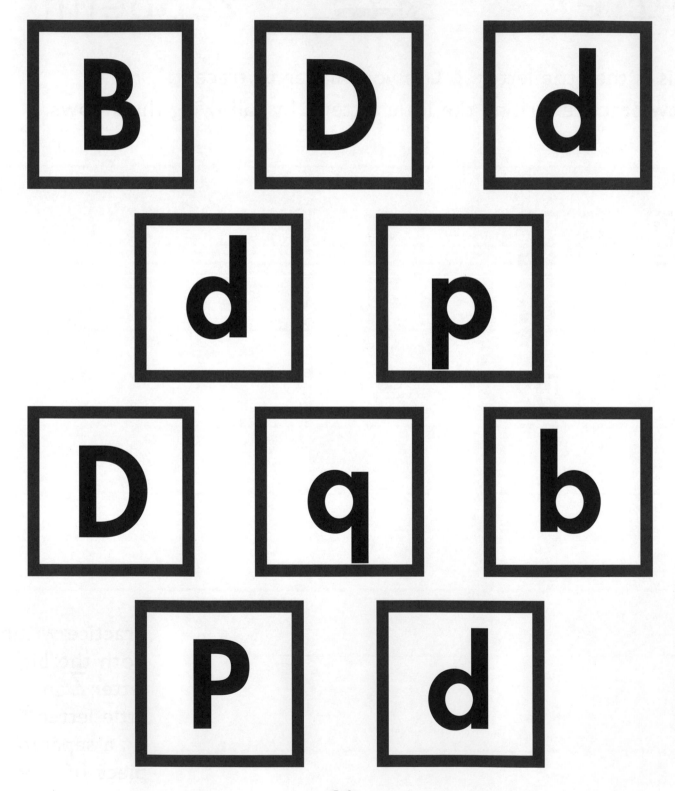

Find the word that begins with F

Which one of these pictures begins with the letter **F** ?
Draw a circle around it.

The Letter T

Each of these stars has a different letter inside it. Color only the stars where you find either the big letter **T** or little letter **t**.

The Letter S

Circle the three things that begin with the letter S.

The Letter Q

Each of these diamonds has a different letter inside it. Color only the diamonds where you find either the big letter Q or little letter q.

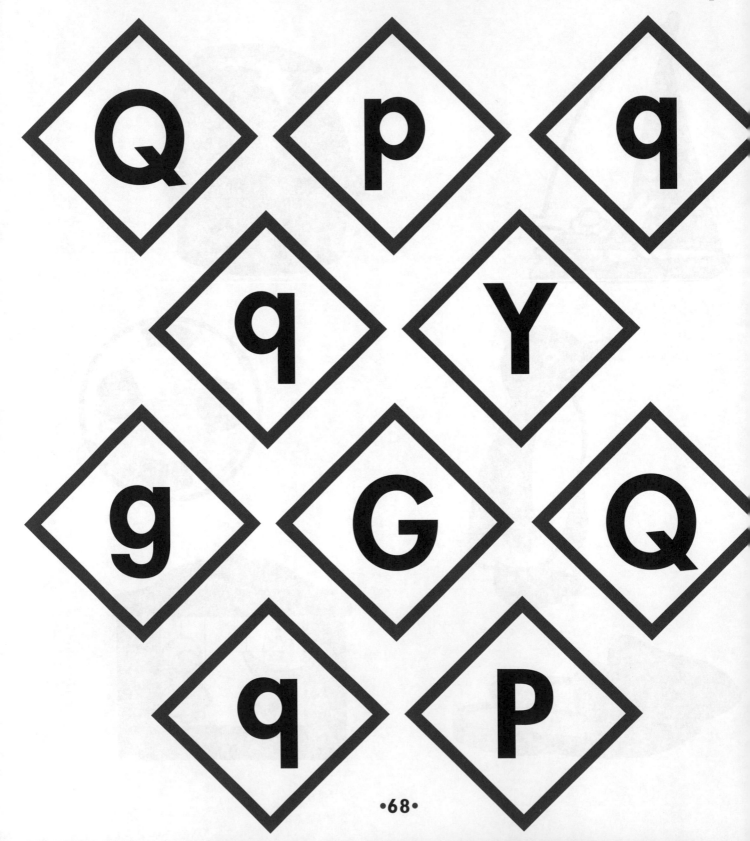

The Letter P

Circle the three things that begin with the letter **P**.

The Letter N

Each of these rectangles has a different letter inside it. Color only the rectangles where you find either the big letter N or little letter n.

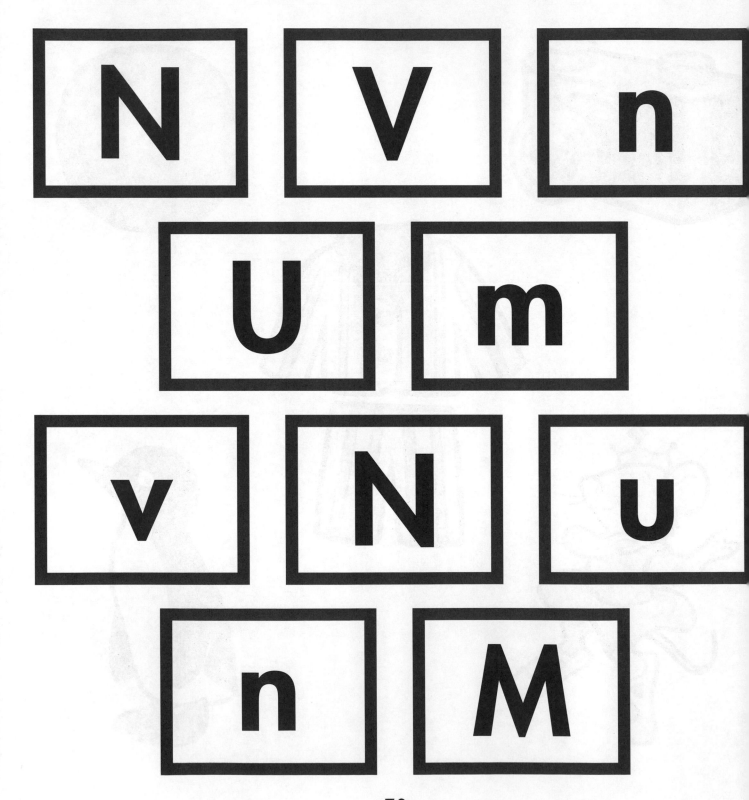

The Letter M

Circle the three things that begin with the letter M.

Words that begin with the letter C

C is for Cat. Can you find a cat on this page? Draw a circle around it.

C is for Camera. Where is the camera? Draw a square around it.

C is for Coat. Brrr, it's cold. Can you point to the coat on this page?

The Letter B

Circle the three things that begin with the letter **B**.

The Letter R

Circle the three things that begin with the letter R.

The Letter H

Each of these circles has a different letter inside it. Color only the circles where you find either the big letter **H** or little letter **h**.

The Letter J

Each of these ovals has a different letter inside it. Color only the ovals where you find either the big letter J or little letter j.

Sound the Letters

Say the name of each picture.
Draw a line to connect each picture on the left
with the picture on the right that begins with the same sound.

P

C

S

The Letter L

Circle the three pictures that begin with the letter L.

Words that begin with the letter G

G is for Goat. Can you find a goat on this page? Draw a circle around it.

G is for Grapes. Where are the grapes? Draw a square around them.

G is for Gorilla. Can you point to the gorilla on this page?

The Letter W

Each of these squares has a different letter inside it. Color only the squares where you find either the big letter **W** or little letter **w**.

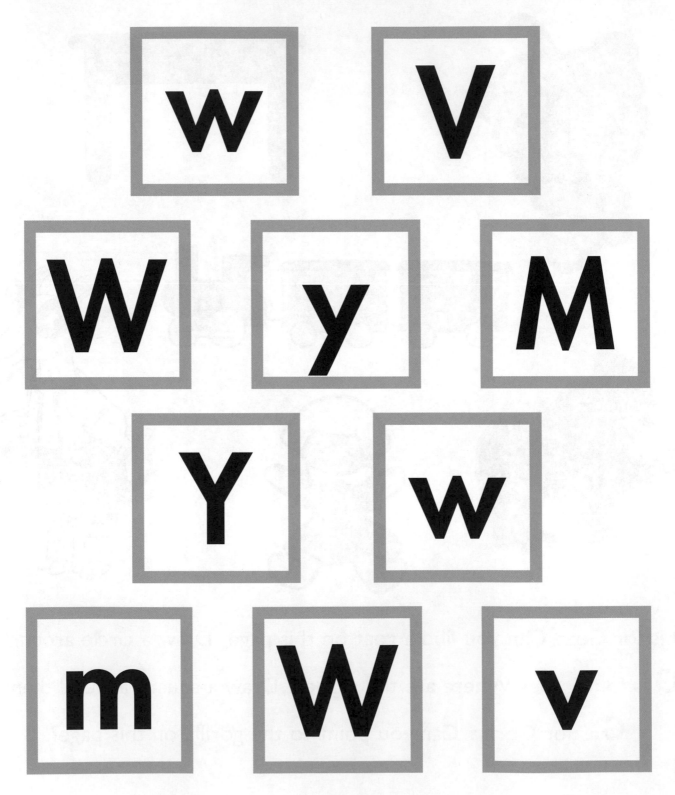

Find the Missing Letters

Fill in the missing letters to complete the words.

do_

c_t

_ow

pi_

Circle The Letter A

Circle all of the things that begin with the letter **A**.

Numbers & Counting

One to Ten

1 ONE

2 TWO

3 THREE

4 FOUR

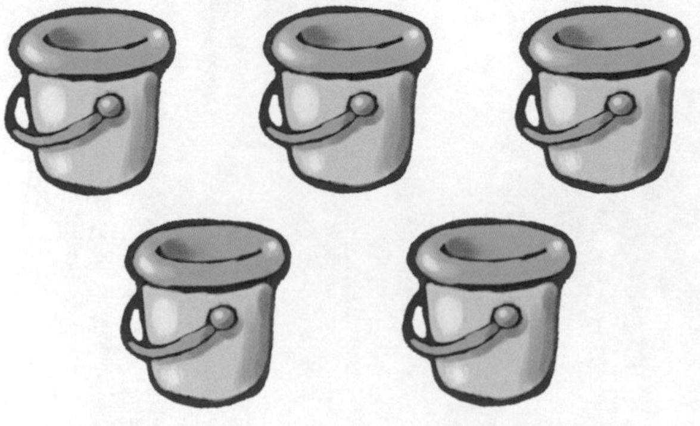

5 FIVE

 **6** SIX

 **7** SEVEN

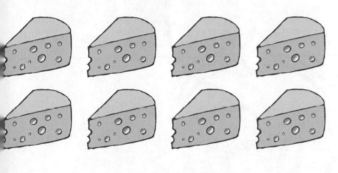 **8** EIGHT

 **9** NINE

 **10** TEN

Color ONE cat.

Carefully write the number ONE below
by following the dotted lines.

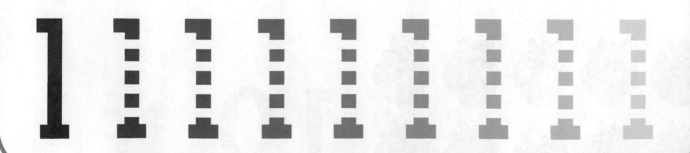

The Number **2**   **TWO**

Color TWO ladybugs.

Write the number TWO below by following the dotted lines.

The Number 3 THREE

Color THREE crabs.

Write the number THREE below
by following the dotted lines.

3 3 3 3 3

The Number 4   FOUR

Color FOUR grasshoppers.

Write the number FOUR below by following the dotted lines.

The Number 5   FIVE

Color FIVE irons.

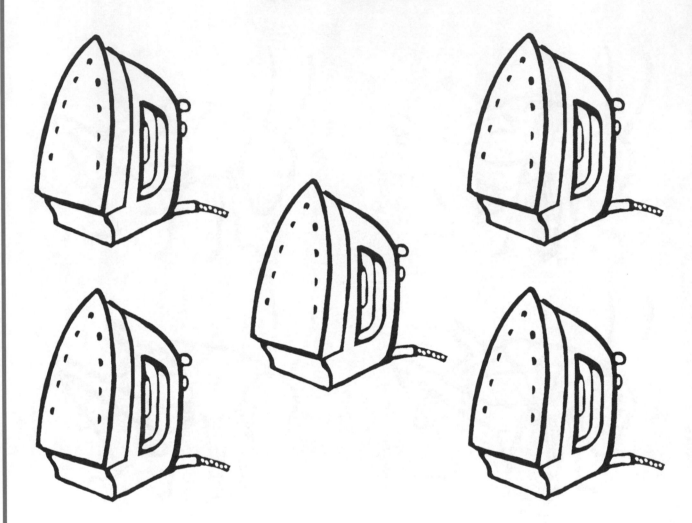

Write the number FIVE below by following the dotted lines.

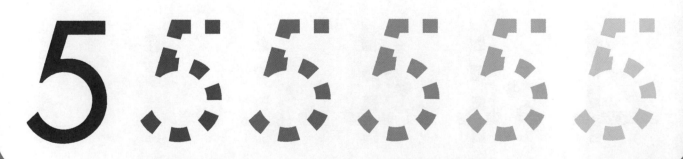

Color SIX seahorses.

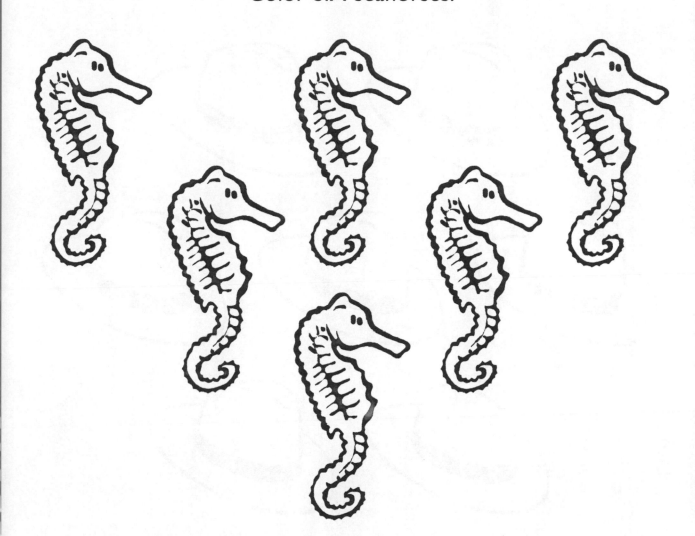

Write the number SIX below by following the dotted lines.

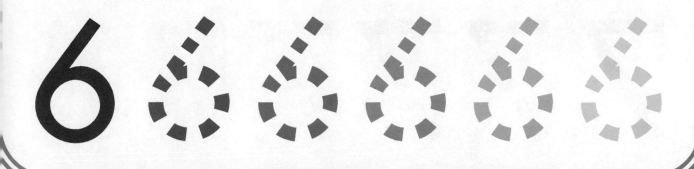

Numbers & Counting

The Number **7**   SEVEN

Color SEVEN hats.

Write the number SEVEN below by following the dotted lines.

7 7 7 7 7 7

The Number 8   EIGHT

Color EIGHT phones.

Write the number EIGHT below by following the dotted lines.

The Number 9 NINE

Color NINE acorns.

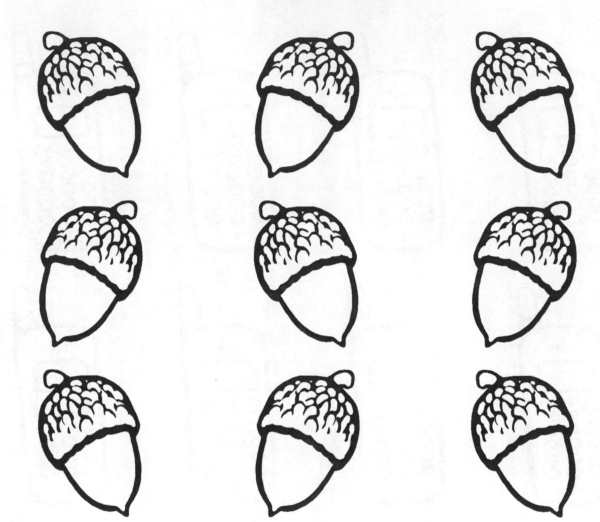

Write the number NINE below by following the dotted lines.

The Number 10   TEN

Color TEN turtles.

Write the number TEN below by following the dotted lines.

Let's Count

1 Dragon

2 Mice

3 Apples

4 Frogs

5 Bees

to TEN

6
Snails

7
Pineapples

8
Penguins

9
Cherries

10
Stars

Play with numbers

Count each object and write the correct number in the box.

WINDMILLS

HEARTS

Play with numbers

Count each object and write the correct number in the box.

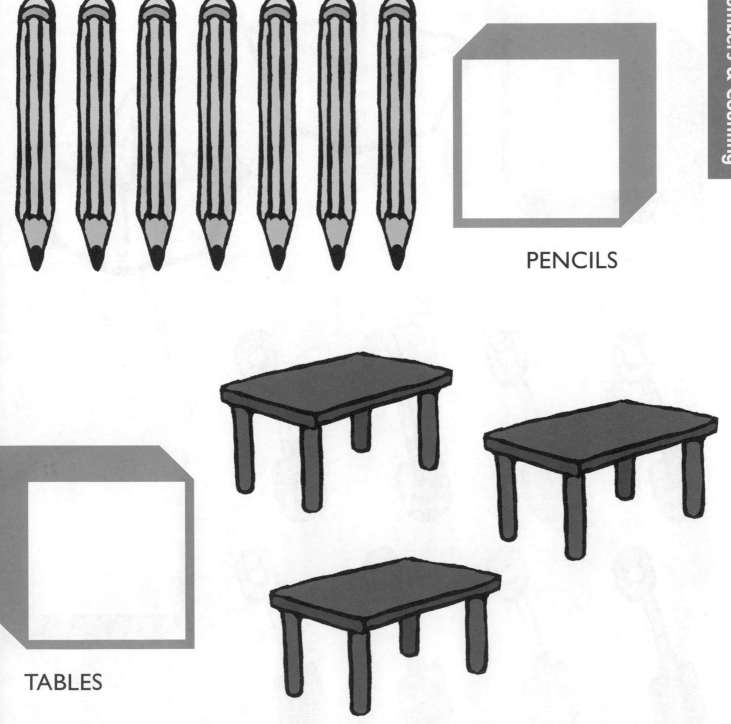

PENCILS

TABLES

•99•

Play with numbers

Count each object and write the correct number in the box.

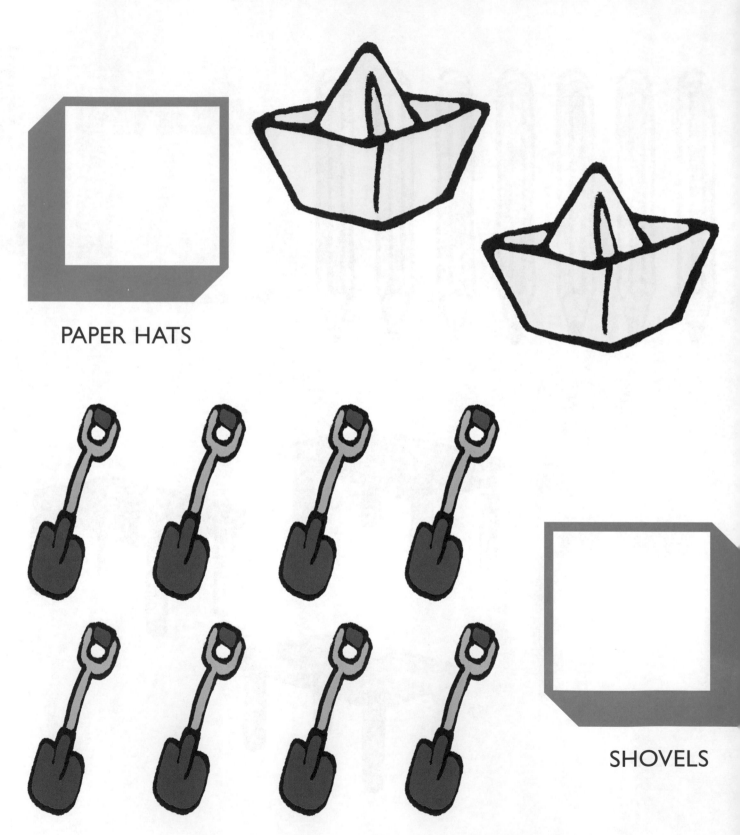

PAPER HATS

SHOVELS

Your Fingers

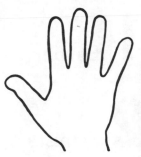

First count all of your fingers. Now place your hand on the page and use a pencil to trace around it. One, two, three, four, five fingers on each hand! How many fingers do you have on both hands?

Now count your toes. How many toes do you have?

Count from ONE

1 Barber

2 Pianists

3 Teachers

4 Fishermen

5 Reporters

6 Explorers

7 Firefighters

8 Chefs

9 Farmers

10 Photographers

to TWENTY

11 Doctors

12 Waiters

13 Astronauts

14 Architects

15 Tailors

16 Singers

17 Policemen

18 Magicians

19 Clowns

20 Ballerinas

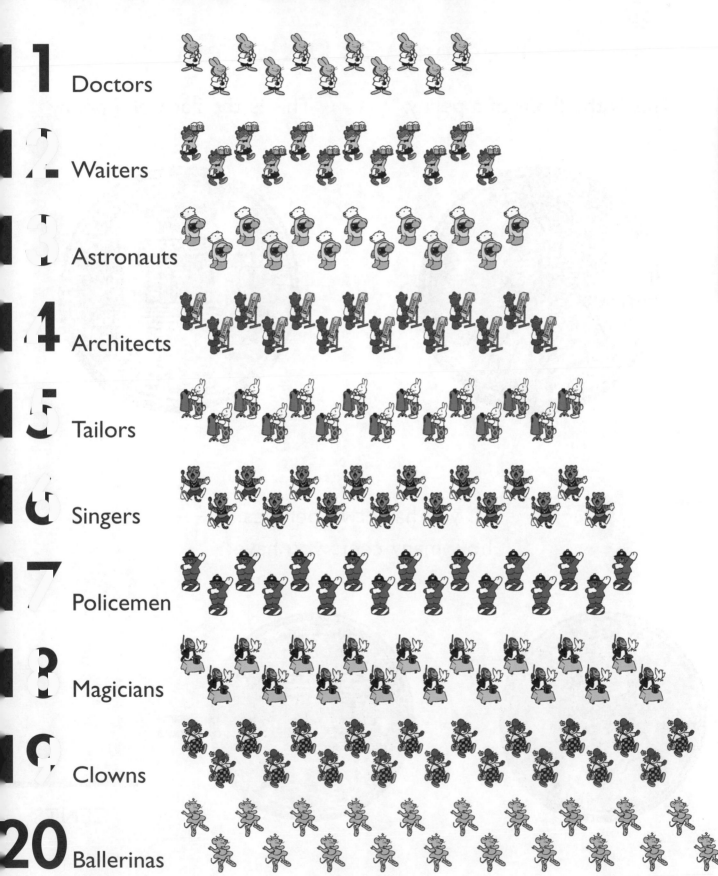

The Penny

One Penny is ONE Cent

This is the front of a penny.

This is the back of a penny.

If you have two pennies,
how many cents you have?

CENTS

The Nickel

One Nickel is FIVE Cents

This is the front of a nickel.   This is the back of a nickel.

If you have one nickel and one penny
how many cents do you have?

_____ CENTS

The Dime

One Dime is TEN Cents

This is the front of a dime.   This is the back of a dime.

If you have one nickel and one dime
how many cents do you have?

_____

CENTS

The Quarter

One Quarter is TWENTY-FIVE Cents

This is the front of a quarter.

This is the back of a quarter.

If you have one quarter and one penny
how many cents do you have?

+

=

_____

CENTS

Let's Learn How To Count Money

One dime equals 2 nickels.

One quarter equals 2 dimes plus 1 nickel.

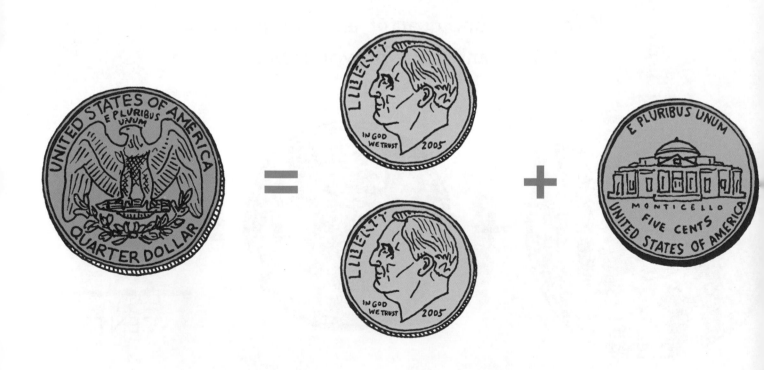

COUNT THE COINS IN THE PIGGY BANK

Count the number of coins in each piggy bank
and write the answer on the line below.

BONUS: Can you say
how much money is
in each piggy bank?

Counting Money

One quarter equals 5 nickels.

 =

One quarter equals 3 nickels and 1 dime.

 =   +

One quarter equals 5 pennies and 2 dimes.

 =    +

One quarter equals 4 nickels and 5 pennies.

 =   +

Addition

Count how many spots there are on the back of each ladybug
and then write down the correct number.

Addition

Draw some dots on the back of the empty ladybugs.
Then add the dots you have drawn to the dots shown on
the other ladybugs. Write the answer next to each picture.

Colors

The Color **Red**

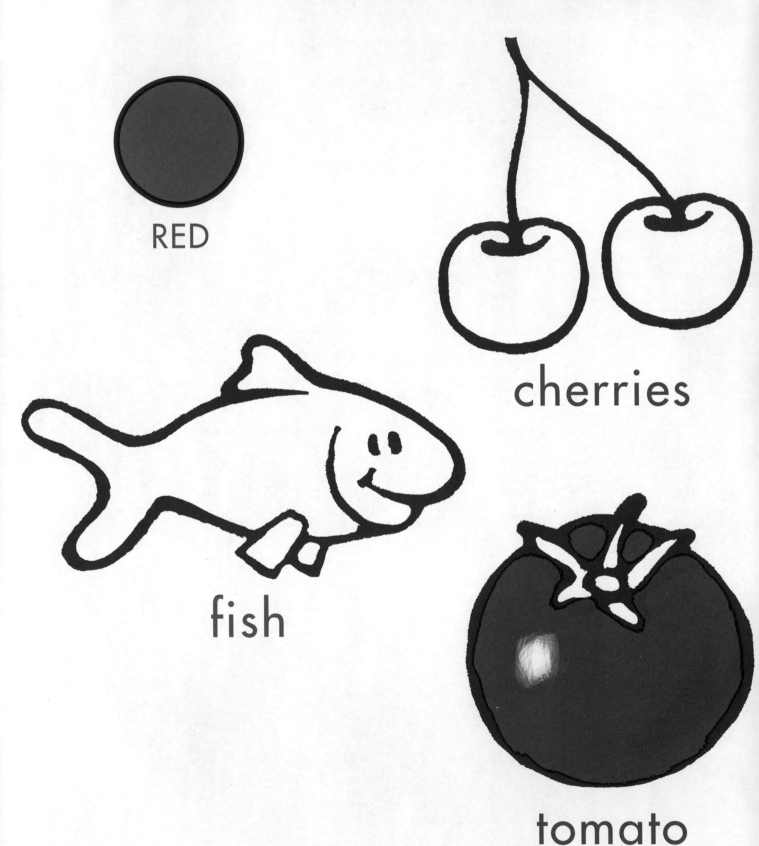

RED

cherries

fish

tomato

Color everything on these pages RED and then say the name of each object.

strawberry

tractor

ladybug

The Color **Blue**

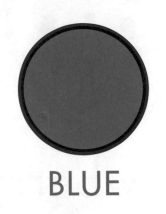

BLUE

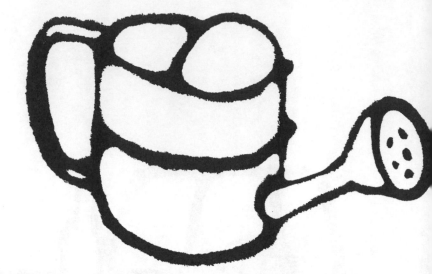

watering can

jeans

scissors

Color everything
on these pages BLUE
and then say the
name of each object.

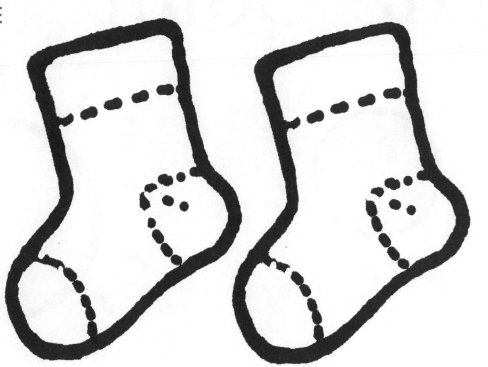

socks

helicopter

The Color Yellow

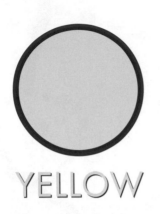

YELLOW

sun

grain

yellowjacket

Color everything on these pages YELLOW
and then say the name of each object.

tiger

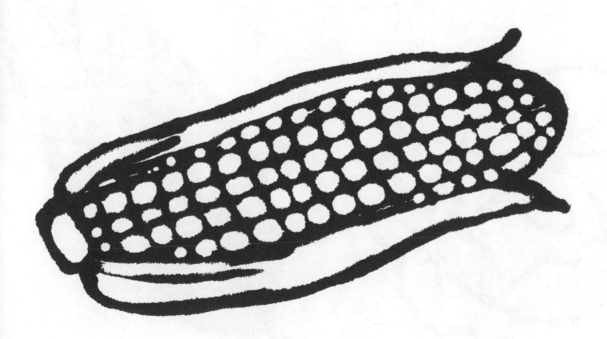

corn

The Color Green

GREEN

peas

lettuce

leaf

Color everything on these pages GREEN
and then say the name of each object.

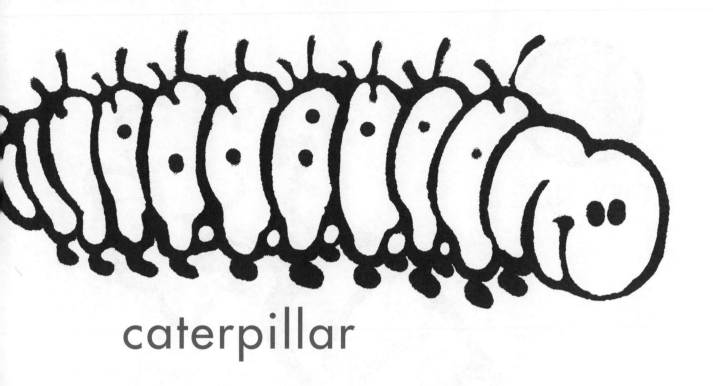

caterpillar

frog

The Color Orange

ORANGE

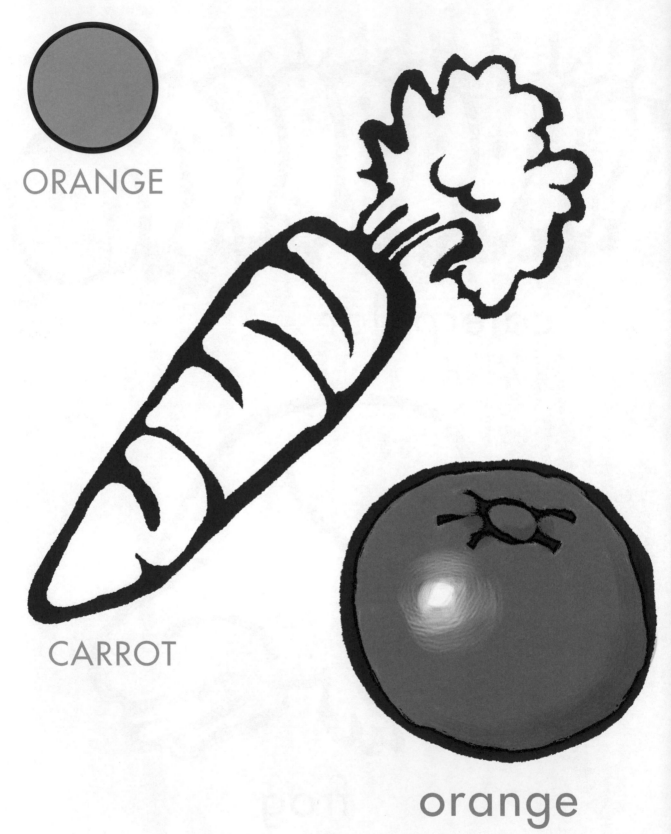

CARROT

orange

Color everything on these pages ORANGE and then say the name of each object.

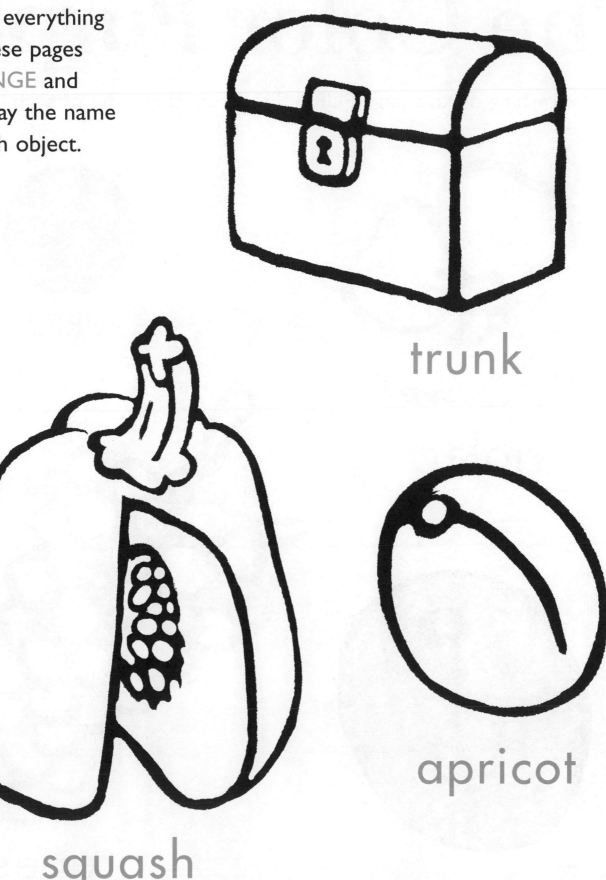

trunk

squash

apricot

Colors

The Color Purple

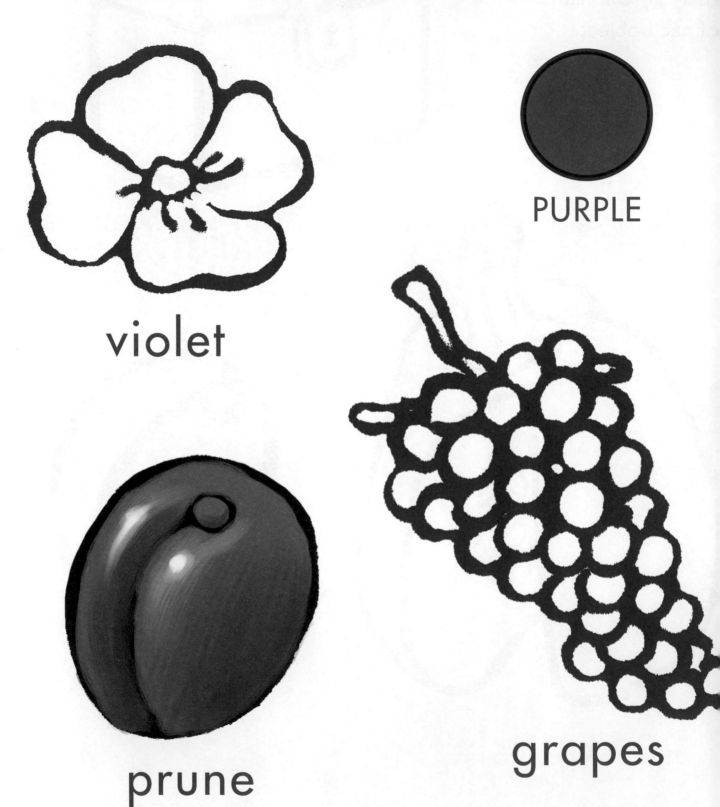

violet

PURPLE

prune

grapes

The Color Brown

Color everything on this page BROWN then say the name of each object.

BROWN

horse

chestnuts

chocolate

The Color White

Everything on this page is WHITE. Say the name of each object.

WHITE

cloud

snowman

dove

The Color **Black**

Color everything on this page BLACK then say the name of each object.

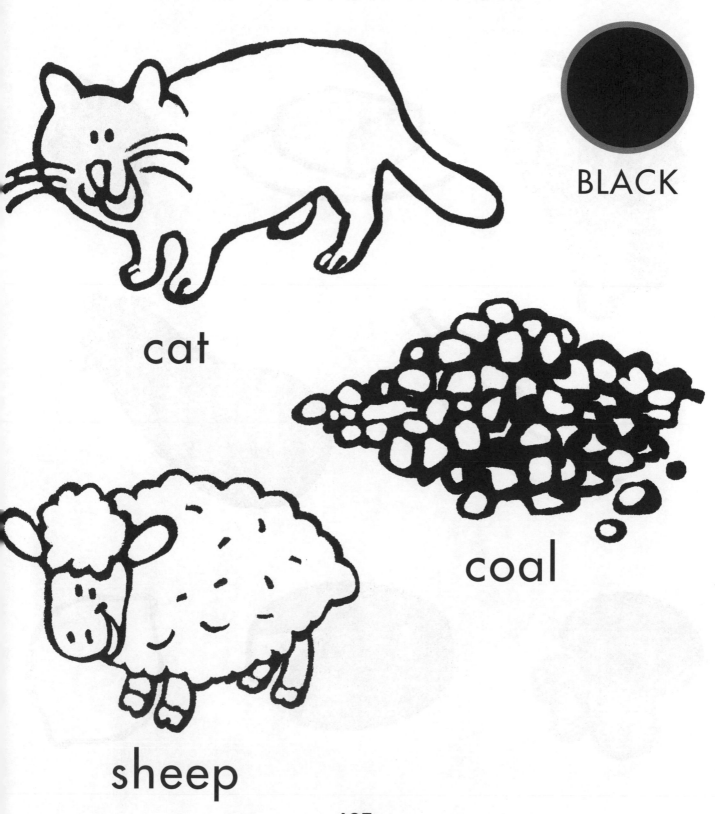

BLACK

cat

coal

sheep

Yellow

Circle all of the foods that are YELLOW.

White

Circle all of the foods that are WHITE.

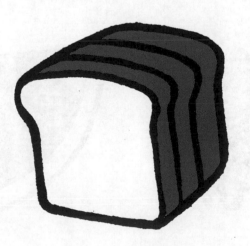

Red

Circle all of the foods that are RED.

Green

Circle all of the foods that are GREEN.

What Color?

"What delicious grapes!"

What color are the grapes?
If you know, write it in the box.

You Can Color

… and now, color the picture below using all of the colors.

Fruits & Vegetables

Put a red circle around the fruits and a green circle around the vegetables.

"Boy, am I hungry!"

Let's Color

Color all of the vegetables and fruits on this page. Make sure that you match the colors on the opposite page.

"What a delicious apple!"

What Color?

What color are the objects on this page? If you know, write it in the box.

·136·

Time to Color

Color the pictures on this page.

"Let's go to the park and play!"

What will you draw?

Draw and color anything you want in the box below.

FRUIT

Circle in RED the fruits you eat during the summer and in BLUE the fruits you eat in the fall.

What is your favorite fruit?

•139•

You Can Color

Color the pictures below any way you like.

COLORS

These objects are different colors.
Point to each one and say its color out loud.

You Can Color

Color the pictures below any way you like.

What Color?

What color are the
objects on this page?
If you know, write it
in the box.

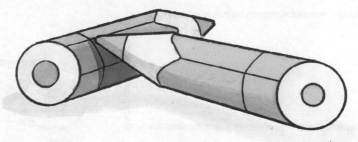

What Color?

What color are the
objects on this page?
If you know, write it
in the box.

Color the Eggs

Color the biggest egg YELLOW,
the medium-sized egg BLUE,
and the smallest egg RED.

Which animal makes the biggest egg?

COLORS

These objects are three different colors.
Point to each one and say its color out loud.

Orange

Circle all of the foods that are ORANGE.

Play with Colors

Color the picture with all of the colors you have learned.

Colors

What Color?

What color are the mice pointing to? Is it the same as the other things on this page? If you know what color it is, write it in the box below.

Shapes

The SQUARE

Find the SQUARE in the picture and color it RED.

•153•

The RECTANGLE

Find the RECTANGLE in the picture and color it BLUE.

The **TRIANGLE**

Find the TRIANGLE in the picture and color it PURPLE.

Shapes

Play with Shapes

A shape is hidden in each picture.
Complete the picture by following the dotted line.
When you are done, say the name of the shape out loud.

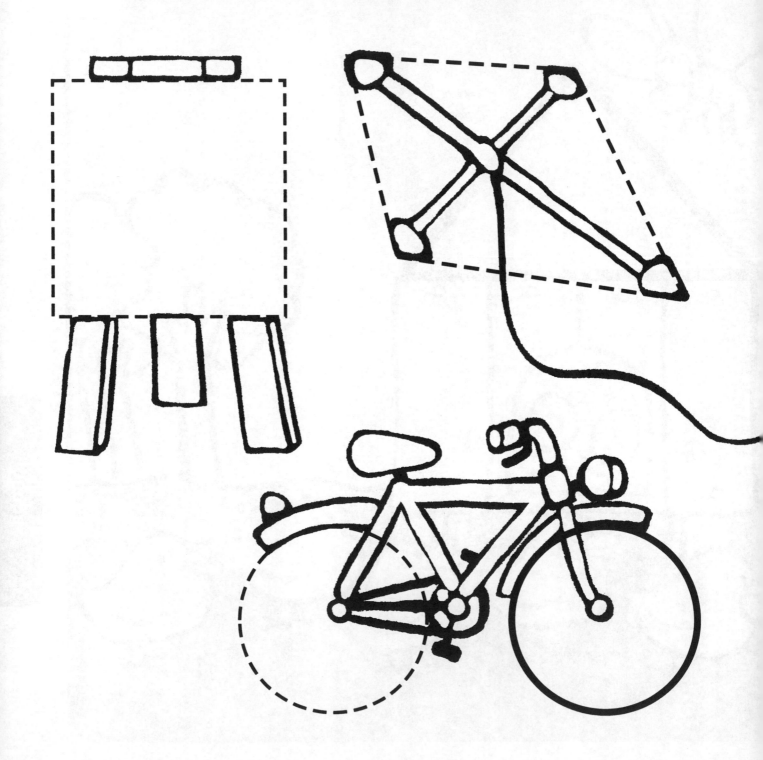

Rectangle

Color the three RECTANGLES on this page.

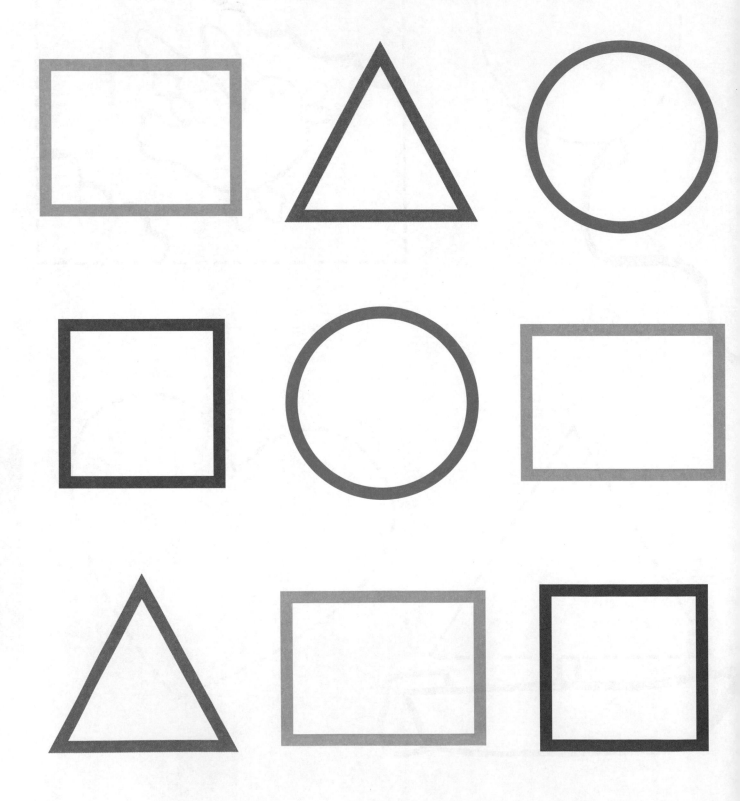

Triangle

Color the three TRIANGLES on this page.

The OVAL

Find the OVAL in the picture and color it ORANGE.

Circle

Color the three CIRCLES on this page.

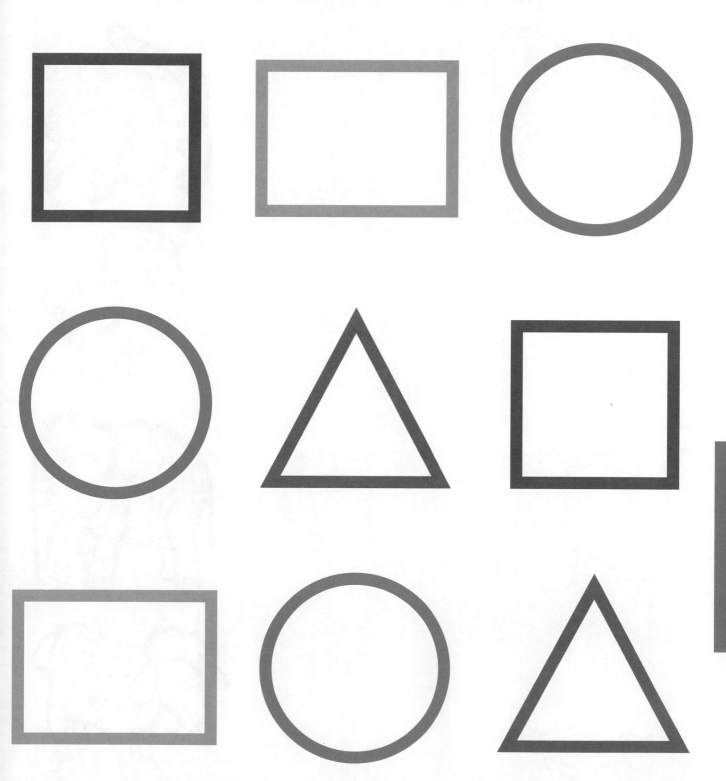

Shapes

•163•

Match the Shapes

Draw lines to match the shapes to the animals.

Square

Color the three SQUARES on this page.

The DIAMOND

Find the DIAMOND in the picture and color it GREEN.

SHAPES

Carefully look at the three different shapes below.
Circle the triangles with a RED crayon, the circles with
a BLUE crayon, and the squares with a PURPLE crayon.

Hidden Shapes

Color the spaces that have dots and find out
which characters are hiding in each of these pictures.

SHAPES

Carefully look at the three different shapes below.
Circle the stars with a YELLOW crayon, the ovals with
a GREEN crayon, and the rectangles with an ORANGE crayon.

Circle the Circles

Circle all of the things that are round on this page.
Then color them.

Match the Shapes

Look carefully at the shapes of the balloons that the clown is holding. Using a RED crayon color the shape that matches the pig. Using a BLUE crayon color the shape that matches the rabbit. Using a BROWN crayon color the shape that matches the bear.

Sizes

Comparisons

Opposites

Same Size

Look at the pictures in each box.
Circle the pictures that are the **same** size.

Big and Bigger

Look at the pictures below.
In each row, circle the picture that is BIGGER than the others.

 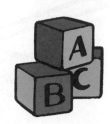  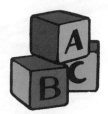

Which is Different?

Look at these pairs carefully.
Circle the pairs that don't quite match.

Play with the Chicks

Each little chick has another little chick that is exactly like it, except for ONE. Can you find the little chick that is different from all of the others?

BIG and little

A tiger is **BIG**.   A kitten is **little**.

Look at the pictures in each row. Circle the one that is little.

Find the Difference

One of these presents is different from the rest.
Circle the one that is different.

Same and Different

Circle the one object in each row that is NOT the same as the others.

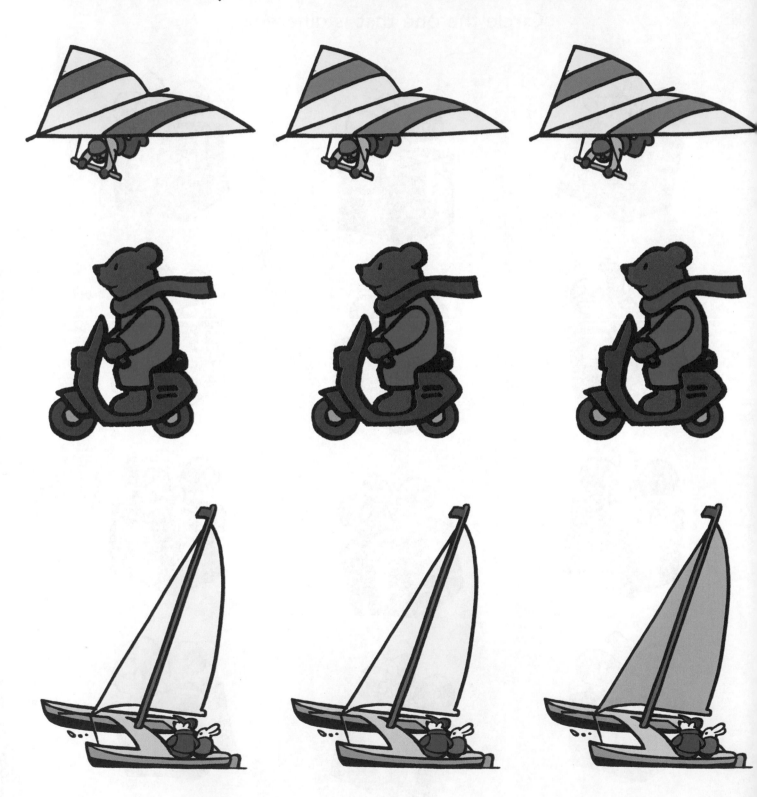

What a Difference

There are four differences between the two pictures of tigers. Can you find them all?

Tall and Short

Teddy has many friends: some of them are TALLER than he is, some are SHORTER, and some are the SAME height.

Look at each picture below and say out loud whether Teddy is TALLER, SHORTER, or the SAME as his friend.

"Hello, Miss Giraffe!"

Above and Below

What animals are under the park bench?

What animal is on top of the bench?

What animal is in front of the bench?

What animal is behind the bench?

"Hello, Mr. Elephant!"

Sizes Comparisons and Opposites

What a Difference

Help Chris the Investigator find the
five differences between the two robots.

OPPOSITES

Look carefully at the pictures below.
What is the opposite of SLOW? What is the opposite of LONG?
Complete the words that are OPPOSITES.

SLOW   FAST

LONG

SHORT

OPPOSITES

Look carefully at the pictures below.
What is the opposite of CLEAN? What is the opposite of SHORT?
Complete the words and then color the pictures.

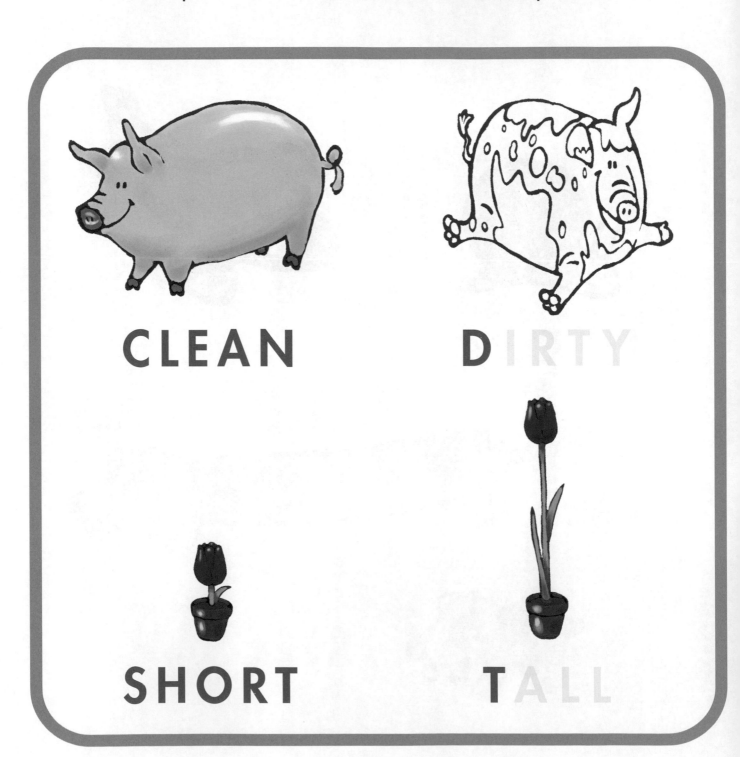

CLEAN

DIRTY

SHORT

TALL

OPPOSITES

Look carefully at the pictures below.
What is the opposite of EMPTY? What is the opposite of THIN?
Complete the words that are OPPOSITES.

EMPTY

FULL

THIN

FAT

OPPOSITES

Look carefully at the pictures and draw a line
connecting each word to its opposite.

FAT

DRY

SHORT

CLOSED

LONG

THIN

OPEN

WET

OPPOSITES

Look carefully at the pictures and draw a line
connecting each word to its opposite.

BIG

TALL

SHORT

EMPTY

SMALL

CLEAN

FULL

DIRTY

OPPOSITES

Say out loud what the opposites are in each pair of pictures.

OPPOSITES

Say out loud what the opposites are in each pair of pictures.

OPPOSITES

Look carefully at the pictures below.
What is the opposite of OPEN? What is the opposite of WET?
Complete the words and then color in the pictures.

OPEN

CLOSED

WET

DRY

OPPOSITES

Look carefully at the pictures below.
What is the opposite of EMPTY? What is the opposite of CLOSED?
Complete the words that are OPPOSITES.

EMPTY   FULL

CLOSED   OPEN

OPPOSITES

Look carefully at the pictures below.
What is the opposite of LITTLE? What is the opposite of OVER?
Complete the words that are OPPOSITES.

LITTLE   BIG

OVER   UNDER

Combinations

What Goes Together?

Circle the two pictures in each row that belong together.

Combinations

Circle the two pictures in each row that belong together.

What Goes Together?

Circle the two pictures in each row that belong together.

Combinations

Circle the two pictures in each row that belong together.

Combinations

Circle the two pictures in each row that belong together.

Match the Hat With the Shirt

Draw a line from each hat to the shirt that matches it.

•201•

Connect the Objects

Oil is made from olives, wine is made from… ?
Draw a line connecting every product to where it comes from.

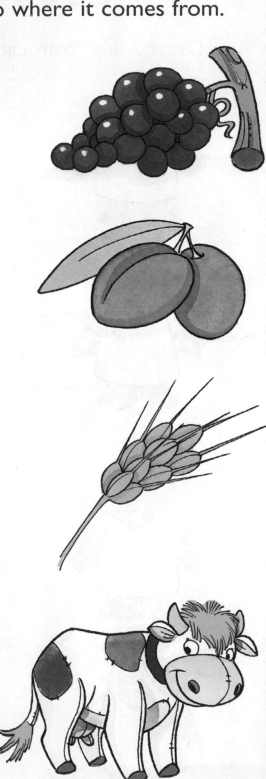

Combinations

Circle the two pictures in each row that belong together.

Combinations

Circle the two pictures in each row that belong together.

Combinations

Circle the two pictures in each row that belong together.

Combinations

Circle the two pictures in each row that belong together.

Our World

Things in Our House

ATTIC

BEDROOM

BATHROOM

KITCHEN

LIVING ROOM

You can find most of these things in your house.
Say out loud the room in which each one belongs.

Bed

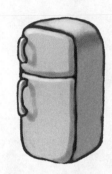

Refrigerator

Bathtub

Bookcase

Couch

Trunk

Dresser

Table

The Seasons

The four seasons are WINTER, SPRING, SUMMER and FALL.

What season does each picture show? Write the correct name under each.

-- -- -- --

-- -- -- --

What do you like to eat?

Circle all of the things on this page that you can eat.

My House

Walk around your house and count how many of each of the following things you have.

 LAMPS

 BEDS

 CHAIRS

 COUCHES

 TELEVISIONS

 RADIOS

 REFRIGERATORS

 TABLES

 SINKS

 BATHTUBS

Fall & Winter

Here are pictures of FALL and WINTER.
How many differences can you find between the pictures?

Winter

Fall

Spring & Summer

Here are pictures of SPRING and SUMMER.
How many differences can you find between the pictures?

Spring

Summer

My Family

Circle all of the members of your family on this page.

My Telephone Number

First connect the dots, beginning with the number one.

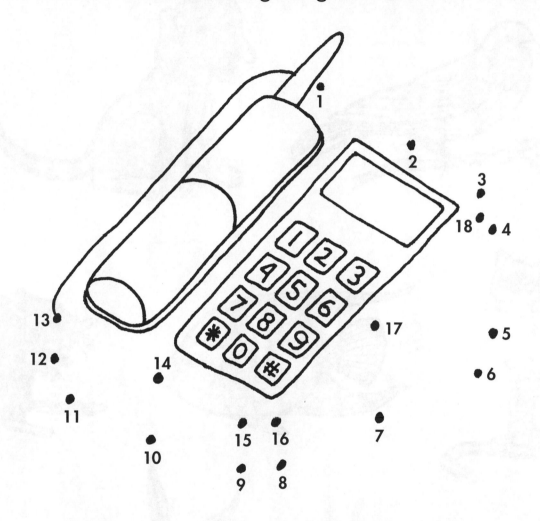

Now write down your telephone number.

(_ _ _) _ _ _ - _ _ _ _

Very good! Now don't forget it, as you may
need to call your home one day.

My Favorite Pets

On this page are several animals that make wonderful pets.
Which of these would be your favorite pets?

Time to Eat

Circle the items that belong on the table.

What's in Your House?

Look carefully at everything inside the house.
Can you find all of the things that you see below?

CHAIR

COUCH

CLOSET

BED

DRAWERS

CRIB

TOILET

STOVE

FIREPLACE

TELEVISION

Let's go to the Beach

Circle all of the things you would take to the beach.

It's Cold Outside

Circle all of the clothing you would wear
if it was snowing and very cold outside.

Find the Tools

The **police officer, farmer, mail carrier, gardener, architect,** and **astronaut** need tools to do their work. Draw a line to what each of them needs.

Match the Jobs

Can you name the jobs of everyone on this page?
Draw a line to match the word with the picture.

Artist

Soccer Player

Chef

Firefighter

Pianist

Doctor

Singer

Explorer

Match the Jobs

Can you name the jobs of everyone on this page?
Draw a line to match the word with the picture.

Barber

Ballerina

Photographer

Clown

Teacher

Race Car Driver

Mail Carrier

Dressmaker

Match the Jobs

Can you name the jobs of everyone on this page?
Draw a line to match the word with the picture.

Fisherman

Farmer

Magician

Judge

Auto Mechanic

Astronaut

Gardener

Police Officer

Find the Tools

The **musician**, **reporter**, **cement builder**, **photographer**, **soccer player**, and **firefighter** need these tools to do their work. Draw a line to what each of them needs.

Find the Tools

The **dressmaker, artist, chef, ballerina, clown,** and **fisherman** need tools to do their work. Draw a line to what each of them needs.

What is a PAIR?

By saying "PAIR" we mean all of the things that are used in sets of two, such as shoes.

You always buy a **pair** of shoes because you have two feet.

Name the Pairs

Here are some examples of pairs:

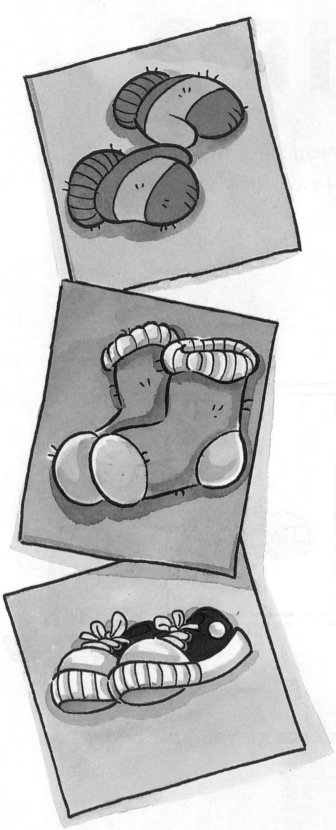

1 Pair of Mittens

1 Pair of Socks

1 Pair of Sneakers

A PAIR OF...

Now that you know what a pair is, circle the pairs on this page.

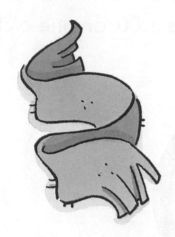

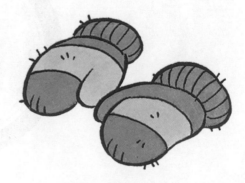

Telling Time

Clocks and watches have a big hand to tell the minutes and a little hand to tell the hour. Look at the picture below. The hour hand is pointing to the 1 and the minute hand is pointing to the 12 (or 0 minutes). It is 1:00, or one o'clock.

In this picture, the hour hand is between numbers 1 and 2, and the minute hand is pointing to the number 30, so it is 1:30, or one thirty.

Telling Time

Each of the four clocks is telling you a different time.
Write down what time it is under each clock.

_ _ : _ _

_ _ : _ _

_ _ : _ _

_ _ : _ _

Telling Time

Each of the four clocks is telling you a different time.
Write down what time it is under each clock.

_ _ : _ _

_ _ : _ _

_ _ : _ _

_ _ : _ _

What to Wear?

Draw lines to match the dressed figures with the right weather.

My Feelings

We can feel many different ways.
Point to each picture and say what feeling it shows.

Sometimes we feel **HAPPY**.
Sometimes we feel **SAD**.

Sometimes we feel **SLEEPY**.
Sometimes we feel **AWAKE**.

Sometimes we feel **SICK**.
Sometimes we feel **HEALTHY**.

Nature

&

Science

Mysterious

Draw a line connecting each animal on this page to its name.

Elephant

Crocodile

Lion

Parrot

Animals

Draw a line connecting each animal on this page to its name.

Kangaroo

Tiger

Giraffe

Penguin

Where do They Live?

Name each of the animals below.
Draw a line connecting each animal to where it lives.

What Noises do the Animals Make?

What does the dog say? What does the cow say? What does the lamb say? Draw a line from each animal to the noise it makes.

Bow Wow

Moo

Meow

Oink

Baa

Who Slides?
Who Hops?

Draw a red circle around the animals that slide and a blue circle around the animals that hop.

Find the Mistake

Oh dear, the elephant has a fox tail! What a mess!
Find the mistake in each picture.

Where do They Live?

The dog lives in the dog house and the horse lives in the ...?
Draw a line connecting each animal to its house.

Where Does Milk Come From ?

Circle the animal that gives us the milk we drink every day.

Where do Animals Live?

Circle the animals whose houses are part of their bodies.

Who is in the Pond?

Who lives above the water and who lives below? Name all of the different animals you see in this picture.

Do They Live Together?

Do these pairs of animals live in the same kind of place?
Mark **YES** or **NO** for each pair below.

☐ **YES**   ☐ **NO**

☐ **YES**   ☐ **NO**

☐ **YES**   ☐ **NO**

☐ **YES**   ☐ **NO**

Who Lives in the Woods?

Circle the three animals that live in the woods.

Find the Animals

Find and circle the animals in the puzzle shown below.

```
A D L S B V M H C
N U D W O E T E O
F C H I C K Y N G
I K A N G A R O O
Q H Y P J Z U R K
P E N G U I N X S
```

chick

kangaroo

penguin

duck

hen

MAMMALS

All of these animals are mammals—except one.
Which one IS NOT a mammal? Circle it.

What Do

Each of the animals below provides us with very useful products.
Draw a line from each animal on this page to the product we get from it.

They Make?

Each of the animals below provides us with very useful products.
Draw a line from each animal on this page to the product we get from it.

WOOL

What Comes From Grain?

Which of the following foods come from **GRAIN**?

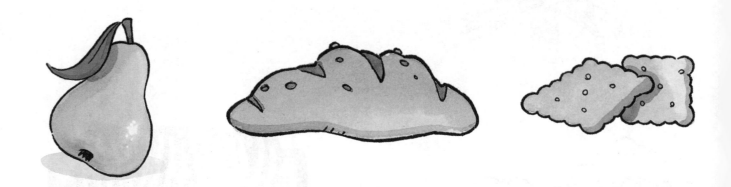

THE FARM

All of these animals except for one live on a farm.
Circle the animal that DOES NOT live on a farm.

Which Animals Fly?

All of the animals below except for one fly.
Circle the animal that DOES NOT fly.

Where Do They Live?

The spider lives in a cobweb, the squirrel lives in a … ?
Connect each animal to where it lives.

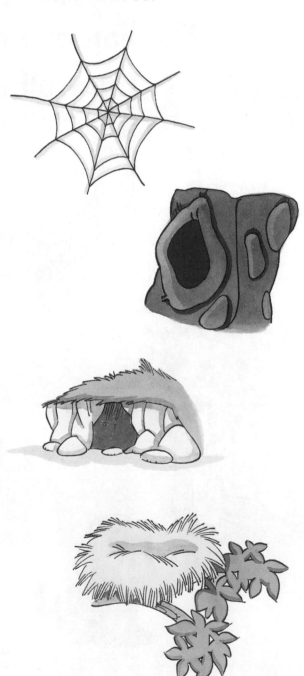

True or False?

Answer out loud TRUE or FALSE to the following statements:

The whale is a mammal.
The ostrich flies.
The lion and the cat are felines.
The wolf is a house pet.

FOOTPRINTS

Draw a line matching each animal to its footprints.
Do your footprints match any of the ones below?

More Farm Animals

All of these animals live on a farm except for **one**.
Pick out the one that DOES NOT live on a farm and circle it.

Where Do They Live?

Which of these animals live in the woods?
Which of these animals live on a farm?
Which of these animals live in the sea?

Where Do They Live?

Which of these animals live in the woods?
Which of these animals live on a farm?
Which of these animals live in the jungle?

Which Ones Are Insects?

There are a lot of creepy crawlers on this page.
An insect has six legs.
Can you find and circle all of the insects on this page?

Where is My Tail?

Draw a line connecting each animal to its tail.

TREE CLIMBERS

The animals in the list below are all good tree climbers.
Find and circle the animals in the puzzle.
The words can be either across or up and down.

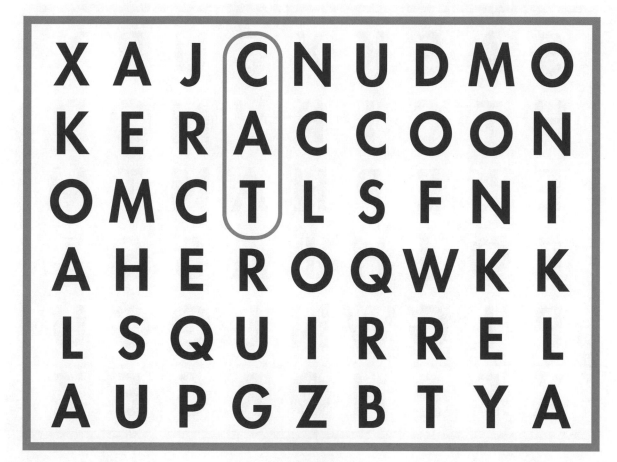

```
X A J C N U D M O
K E R A C C O O N
O M C T L S F N I
A H E R O Q W K K
L S Q U I R R E L
A U P G Z B T Y A
```

monkey   raccoon   koala   cat   squirrel

Animals with Hooves

The animals in the list below all have hooves.
Find and circle the animals in the puzzle.
The words can be either across or up and down.

```
S A S K X E U R Y
H T C I R V N O D
E L E P H A N T M
E O J H I A B S I
P I G W N L Q G U
X F P H O R S E Z
```

rhino

pig

elephant

sheep

horse

More Farm Animals

All of these animals live on a farm except for **one**.
Pick out the one that DOES NOT live on a farm and circle it.

Will it Sink or...

This is a fun experiment to see which objects will sink and which will float.

YOU WILL NEED

Assorted Objects, such as:

- A ball of cotton

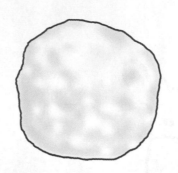

- A penny

- A piece of sponge

- A key

- A toy car

- A spoon

- A rubber band

- A cork

- A large bowl of water
  or
- A sink half filled with water.

...Will it Float?

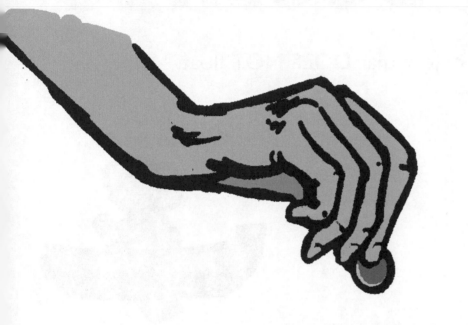

Choose one object at a time, but before you put it in the bowl of water guess whether it will sink or float.

BE CAREFUL AND DON'T PUT ANY OBJECT IN YOUR MOUTH.

What Floats? What Doesn't?

Circle the object that DOES NOT float.

Games

Oh, Oh, Dress George!

Oops! George the Giraffe is only half dressed! Using a pencil, carefully connect the broken lines to complete the picture. Then color the picture any way you like.

Connect the Dots

Aren't these insects pretty? Beginning at the number 1, connect the dots to help them fly. Then color them in!

Games

ACTIONS

Draw a line matching the picture to the activity.

Eat

Go Out

Play

What a Mess!

Penguin hurt his leg, but how? The pictures are out of order.
Put them in the correct order by numbering them 1, 2, 3, 4, and 5,
to show how Penguin broke his leg.

Connect the Dots

Complete the picture by connecting the dots
and then color it in any way you like.

Tic-Tac-Toe

Play this game with a friend.
Take turns placing an "x" or an "o"
on the grid and the first one to
have three in a row (horizontal,
vertical, or diagonal) wins!

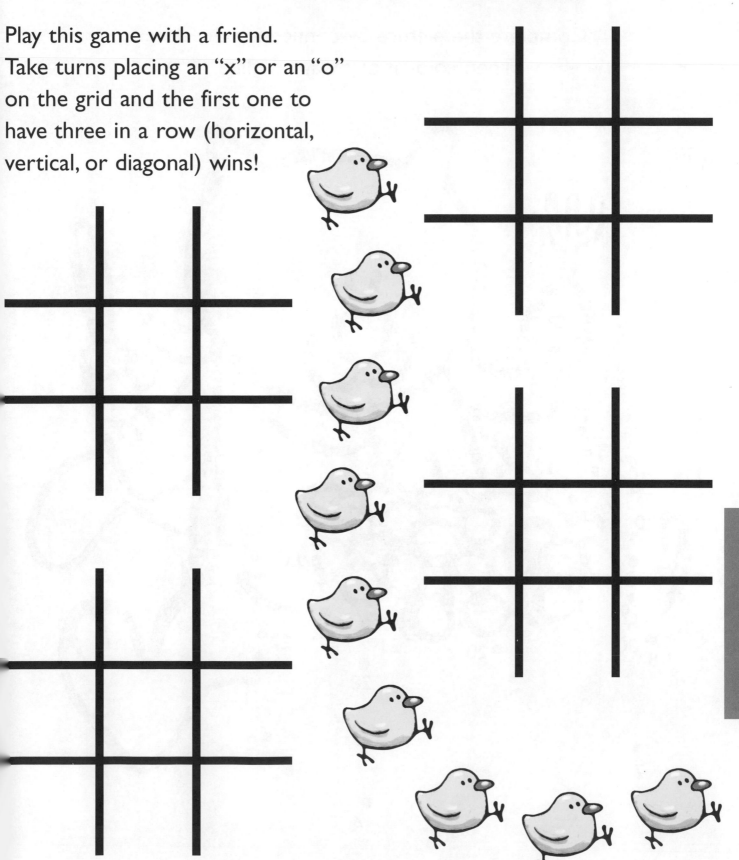

•277•

Connect the Dots

Complete the picture by connecting the dots.
Then color it any way you like.

Follow the Line

Which colored line will lead the baby calf to its mother? Follow it with a pencil or crayon.

•279•

Oh, Oh, Dress Harry!

Oops! Harry the Hippopotamus is only half dressed! Using a pencil, carefully connect the broken lines to complete the picture. Then color the picture any way you like.

Where is Jack-in-the-Box?

Color the spaces that have **blue** dots **blue** and **purple** dots **purple** and find out where Jack-in-the-Box is hiding.

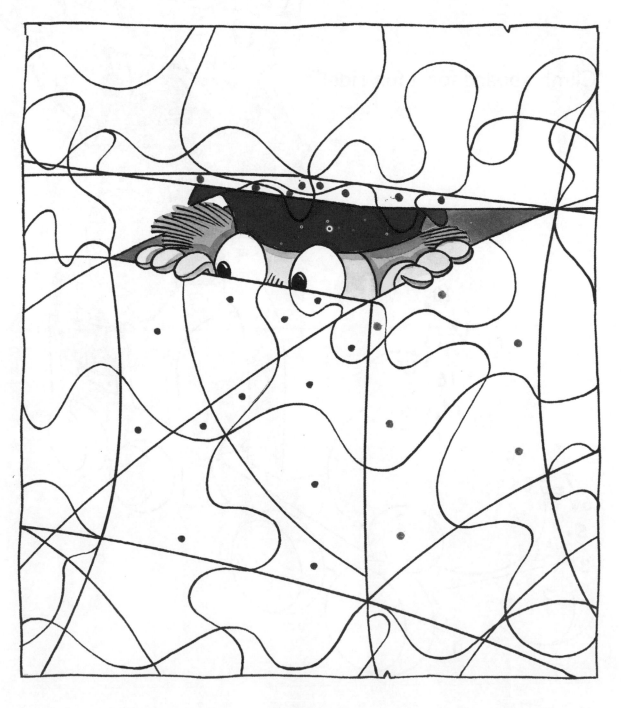

Connect the Dots

Complete the picture by connecting the dots. Then color it any way you like.

"Climb aboard for a fun ride!"

What a Mess!

These pictures are out of order. Put them in order by numbering them 1, 2, 3, and 4, and show what happened when the raccoon tasted some honey.

Connect the Dots

Complete the picture by connecting the dots.
Then color it any way you like.

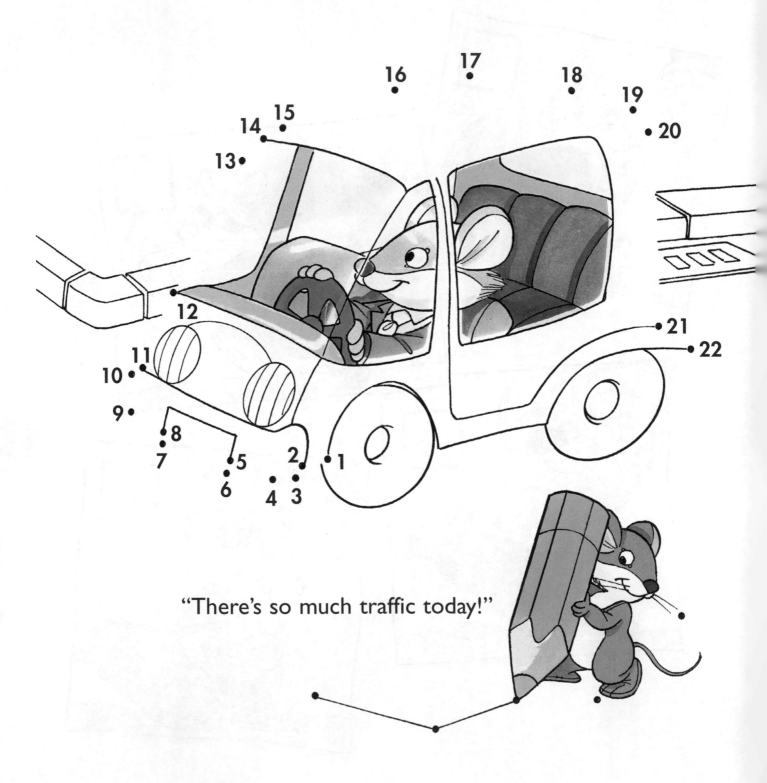

"There's so much traffic today!"

Look and Find

Help Mother Rabbit find the hidden bunnies. How many are there?

"What a mess!"

Games

The Maze

Help the **cat** reach his friend the **mouse**. Draw a red line showing the path that the **cat** must follow.

Let's Play

What a mess! Isabella is tangled up with other strips of paper.
To set her free, color her to the tip of her tail.

"Tommy Bear, help me please!"

"All right, I'll try!"

What a Mess!

These pictures are out of order. Put them in order by numbering them 1, 2, 3, and 4, and show what happened when Anna opened a present.

Help the Policeman

The policeman lost his shadow! Can you help him find it?
One of the three outlines below matches the picture of the policeman.
Circle the correct one.

Games

Match the Objects

Can you guess what the black objects are?
Draw a line from each one to its correct match.

The Hidden Picture

Color the spaces that have dots. Color each one the same color as the dot. Now you know where little tiger is hiding!

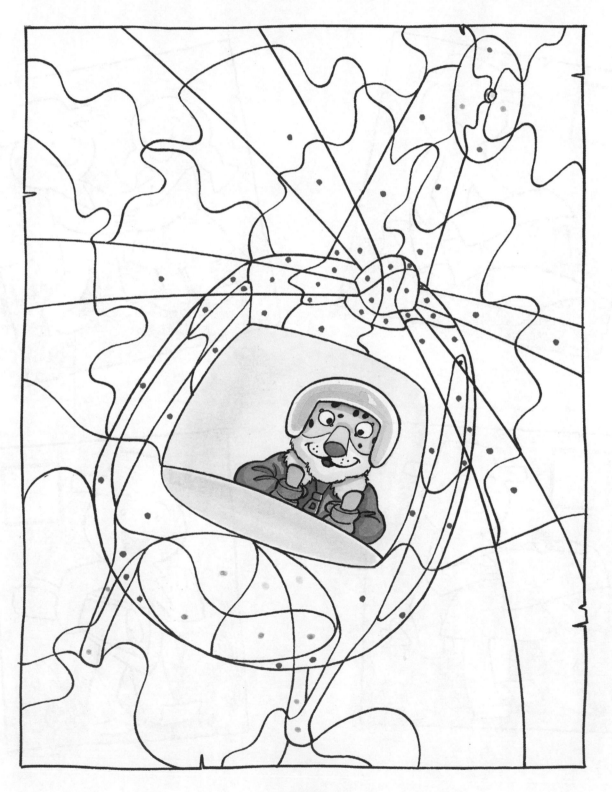

•291•

What a Mess!

These pictures are out of order. Put them in order by numbering them 1, 2, 3, and 4, and show how the paper doll boy made a friend.

LADYBUGS

How many ladybugs are hiding in the picture?
Find and count them.

Games

Draw Your Own **Picture**

Draw whatever you like and color it in, using Mr. Skunk's easel.

"Let's see what you can draw!"

The Hidden Picture

Color the spaces that have dots. Make each one the same color as the dot, and find out what the toy looks like in color.

Games

The Maze

Help the dog reach his friend the crocodile. Draw a red line showing the path that the dog must follow.

Crafts

Let's Make a

Today you can make a horse to play with: but be careful, you will need an adult's help to sew all of the parts together!

YOU WILL NEED:
- a broom
- two buttons
- an old sock
- pink felt fabric
- a pair of scissors
- cotton for stuffing
- a needle and thread
- some yarn

Let's begin, but first get an adult who can help you. Someone has to sew two buttons on the sock for the eyes and two pieces of felt on the sock for the ears. The felt should be cut in the shape shown below.

Hobby Horse

Step 1: Have your grown-up helper sew the ears on the sock.

Step 2: Now, the pieces of yarn must be sewn on to make the horse's mane.

Step 3: When the mane is finished, stuff the sock (or the horse's head) with cotton until it is full.

Step 4: Finally, insert the end of the broomstick into the sock and tie up the bottom with some more yarn.

Now your horse is ready to gallop round wherever you want to take him. Have fun!

Make Your

WHAT YOU WILL NEED:

- 4 cups flour
- 1 1/2 teaspoons salt
- 1 teaspoon alum
- 1 1/2 cups water
- large mixing bowl
- reusable plastic bag
- spoon
- food coloring

Step 1:

Mix the salt, flour, and alum in a large bowl.

Step 2:

Add the water gradually, then the food coloring. Mix all of the ingredients well. You may want to make different colors of clay so separate the mixture into several batches.

Own Clay

Step 3:

Roll and pull and knead the clay, adding just enough water so that it forms a ball.

Step 4:

Wrap the dough in a sealed plastic bag in the refrigerator. When you want to use it, allow the clay to come to room temperature, as it will be easier to form objects.

Now begin to make anything you like.
Would you like to make a bunny? A dog? A dinosaur?
A caterpillar? A snake? Use your imagination and have fun!

STONE

You can begin a collection of "Stone Buddies" that you and your friends can play with when they come to your house.

WHAT YOU WILL NEED:

- a smooth, clean rock
- a brush
- acrylic paint
- glue
- magic markers
- glitter
- googly eyes
- yarn

BUDDIES

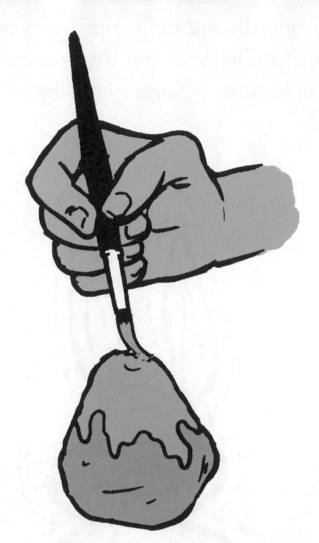

Step 1:
Make sure that your rock
is both clean and dry.
Paint it any color you wish.

Step 2:
When the paint is completely
dry, decorate your rock. You
can glue on googly eyes, glitter,
and some yarn for the hair.

Make as many Stone Buddies as you like.
Have fun with your new friends!

A Family of

Trace the animals and then copy them onto construction paper. Carefully cut out the two circles so that you can stick your fingers into the holes.

WHAT YOU WILL NEED:

- a pencil
- a pair of scissors
- construction paper in different colors
- magic marker pens in different colors with thin tips

Step 1:

Trace the character that you like best on tracing paper.

Step 2:

Carefully cut out your drawing.

Step 3:

Place the cut out drawing on top of a piece of construction paper and carefully cut it so that it matches the tracing paper. Color the shapes to look like the picture.

Step 4:

Cut out the two holes (bottom) where you will put your fingers.

Finger Puppets

Step 5:

Color in your finger puppet any way you like.

Now you have one finished puppet!

Repeat steps 1-5 for the other two characters.
When you finish you will have your own set of puppets.
Now you can make up a story and put on a finger puppet show!

Crafts

Build Your Own

It's a lot of fun to feed the birds and now you can make your own feeder to attract birds to your house. This is also a wonderful gift that you can give to someone special during the holidays.

YOU WILL NEED:
- a pine cone
- string
- peanut butter
- a spoon
- birdseed
- bowl or kitchen sink

To make your bird feeder:

Step 1:
Tie a piece of string around one end of the pine cone.

Step 2:
Scoop some peanut butter from a jar and spread the peanut butter all over the pine cone.

BIRD FEEDER

Step 3:

Pour the birdseed into a bowl. Roll the pine cone in birdseed until all of the peanut butter is covered.

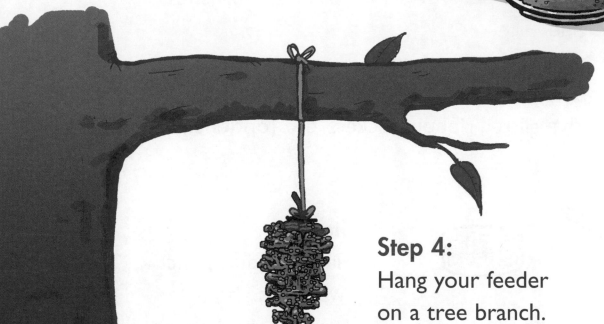

Step 4:

Hang your feeder on a tree branch.

Some birds fly south so that they can stay warm in the winter. However, there are many birds that stay up north and they need help finding food. Feeding birds helps them to live and gives you a chance to watch them. Once you start feeding them please continue to do so because the birds will come to depend on you.

Crafts

A Treasure Box

You can design your own special treasure box in which to keep all of your favorite things. This is also a nice gift.

WHAT YOU WILL NEED:
- two disposable bowls made out of paper or Styrofoam
- twisty tie
- crayons, felt-tip pens, or acrylic paint and brushes
- white glue
- small round button or bead
- paper hole puncher
- decorative glitter, ribbon, stickers, etc. (optional)

Step 1:
Have an adult punch two holes about 1 inch apart through the rims of the two bowls.

Step 2:

Thread a twisty tie through each pair of holes and twist the ends to secure the bowls to each other.

Step 3:

Decorate the box as you please with crayons, markers, or paint. Add stickers or anything else you would like.

Step 4:

Glue the button or bead to the front of the lid to use as a handle to make the opening and closing easier.

Crafts

Make Animals Out of Egg Cartons

This is an easy way to make three different creepy crawlers.

YOU WILL NEED:

- an empty egg carton
- crayons or magic markers
- scissors
- pipe cleaners
- googly eyes or black and white felt

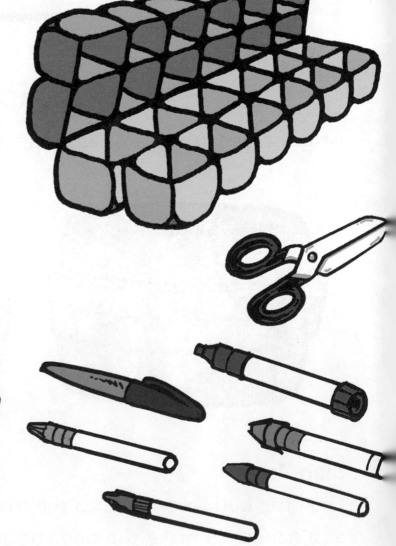

Make a Ladybug

Step 1:

Have an adult help you cut one cup from an egg carton.
Using markers or paint, color the egg carton cup red.
Make sure that it dries well, then, using black paint,
color in the head, and paint some spots on the body.

Step 2:

Have an adult help you make three holes on the side of
each cup, and make two small holes at the top of the head.

Step 3:

Insert a long black pipe
cleaner into each
hole on the
side of the cup
and thread it
through the hole on the
opposite side. These will
make up the legs for the
ladybug. Then cut one pipe
cleaner in half and insert into
the two holes at the top of
the head to make antennae.

Step 4:

Paint on eyes or
glue on googly eyes.

Make a Caterpillar

Step 1:

Separate 4 to 6 cups from an egg carton.

Step 2:

Using the point of a scissors, have an adult make two small holes at one end for the antennae.

Step 3:

Insert pipe cleaners for the antennae.

Step 4:

Add eyes and a mouth and decorate the body using crayons or magic markers.

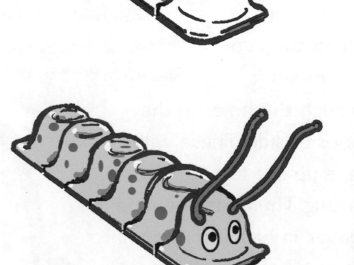

Make a Bat

Step 1:

Separate 3 cups from an egg carton.

Step 2:

Cut out part of the two outside cups to resemble bat wings.

Step 3:

Add eyes and a mouth, and decorate the body.

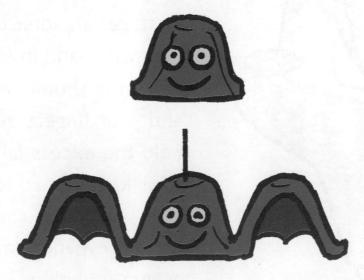

Step 4:

Hang the bat from a string or a rubber band.

Sock Puppets

Sock puppets are fun and simple toys to make. Start by finding an old sock that will fit your hand. Here is the list of materials that you will need to make a very basic sock puppet.

WHAT YOU WILL NEED:

- one old sock
- two buttons for the eyes
- another different color button for the nose
- felt for the pupils
- a needle and thread

Step 1:

First, get an adult to help you. Put your hand in the sock (with the thumb in the heel and your fingers in the toe). Fold the excess fabric above your knuckles to form a ridge. This will create the illusion for the eyeline. Have your grown-up helper tack it down with a needle and thread.

Step 2:

Have your grown-up helper sew on buttons at the eyeline. Cut out circles of paper that will fit inside the buttons and glue them in the center of each button. Or you can use some googly eyes and glue them on instead.

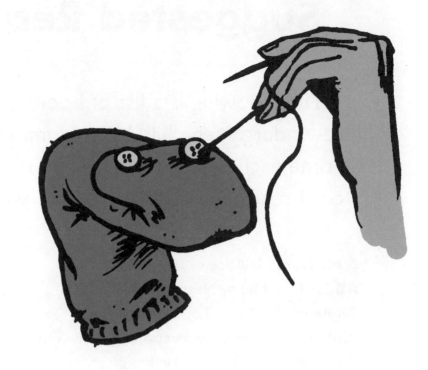

Step 3:

Have your grown-up helper sew on the remaining button for the nose.

If you would like to make other sock puppets you can always add arms, ears, hats, hair (like braids) and other items such as a cape, scarf, and whiskers.

Suggested Reading List

The following is a list of books appropriate for your pre-kindergarten child. We recommend setting aside some time each day to read with your child. The more your child reads, the faster he or she will acquire other skills.

A My Name Is Alice by Jane Bayer

ABC, I Like Me! by Nancy Carlson

All Ready for School by Leone Adelson

Alphabet Under Construction by Denise Fleming

Amazing Graze by Mary Hoffman

Amelia Bedelia by Peggy Parish

Animal Crackers: Nursery Rhymes by Jane Dyer

Antics: An Alphabet Anthology by Catherine Hepworth

Are You My Mother? by Philip Eastman

The Art Lesson by Tomie De Paola

Babushka's Mother Goose by Patricia Polacco

Bear Wants More by Karma Wilson

The Big Dipper by Frankflyn M. Branley

The Big Green Pocketbook by Candice Ranson

Blueberries for Sal by Robert McCloskey

The Cat in the Hat by Dr. Seuss

A Chair for My Mother by Vera B. Williams

Chinese Mother Goose by Robert Wyndham

Click, Clack, Moo: Cows That Type by Doreen Cronin

Clifford the Big Red Dog by Norman Bridwell

Curious George by Hans Augusto Rey

Does the Moon Change Shape? by Meish Goldish

Don't Let the Pigeon Drive the Bus by Mo Willems

Down by the Bay by Raffi

Eensy, Weensy, Spider by May Ann Hoberman

Five Little Monkeys by Eileen Christelow

Frog and Toad Are Friends by Arnold Lobel

Froggy Gets Dressed by Johnathan London

George and Martha by James Marshall

A Giraffe and a Half by Shel Silverstein

The Giving Tree by Shel Silverstein

Green Eggs and Ham by Dr. Seuss

Growing Vegetable Soup by Lois Ehlert

Happy Birthday, America! by Marsha Wilson Chali

Harold and the Purple Crayon by Crockket Johnson

Honeybees by Deborah Heiligman

Horton Hatches the Egg by Dr. Seuss

How Many? How Much? by Rosemary Wells

How the Grinch Stole Christmas by Dr. Seuss

I Know an Old Lady Who Swallowed a Fly by Brian Karas

If You Give a Mouse a Cookie by Laura Joffe Numeroff

If You Take a Mouse to School by Laura Joffe Numeroff

Is It Red? Is It Yellow? Is It Blue? by Tana Hoban

Jumanji by Chris Van Allsburg

Kipper's A to Z: An Alphabet Adventure by Mark Inkpen

A Light in the Attic by Shel Silverstein

Lilly's Purple Plastic Purse by Kevin Henkes

The Little Engine That Could by Watty Piper

The Little House by Virginia Lee Burton

The Little Red Lighthouse and the Great Gray Bridge by Hildegarde H. Swift

Lizards for Lunch-A Roadrunner's Tale by Conrad Storad

Madeline by Ludwig Bemelmans

Make Way for Ducklings by Robert McCloskey

The Man Who Walked Between the Towers by Mordical Gerstein

Math Curse by Jon Scieszka

May Wore Her Red Dress by Merle Peek

Miss Bindergarten Gets Ready for Kindergarten (series) by Joseph Slate

The Mitten by Jan Brett

Mouse Paint by Ellen Stoll Walsh

My First Days of School by Jane Hamilton-Merritt

No, David! by David Shannon

Oh, the Places You'll Go by Dr. Seuss

Olivia by Ian Falconer

One Fish, Two Fish, Red Fish, Blue Fish by Dr. Seuss

One Hungry Monster by Susan Heyboer O'Keefe

Over in the Meadow by John Longstaff

The Paper Bag Princess by Robert Munsch

A Picture Book of Harriet Tubman by David A. Adler

The Polar Express by Chris Van Allsburg

Read-Aloud Rhymes for the Very Young by Jack Prelutsky

Red Leaf, Yellow Leaf by Lois Elhert

School Bus by Donal Crews

The Snowy Day by Ezra Jack Keats

Spot Counts from 1-10 by Eric Hill

Stellaluna by Janell Cannon

The Story of Ferdinand by Munro Leaf

Strega Nona by Tomie de Paola

Sylvester and the Magic Pebble by William Steig

Ten Black Dots by Donald Crews

Ten Seeds by Ruth Brown

Timothy Goes to School by Rosemary Wells

Two Little Trains by Margaret Wise Brown

The Velveteen Rabbit by Margery Williams

Welcome to Kindergarten by Anne Rockewell

What Do You Do With a Tail Like This? by Steve Jenkins

Where the Sidewalk Ends by Shel Silverstein

Where the Wild Things Are by Maurice Sendak

Who Said Red? by Mary Serfozo

The Z Was Zapped by Chris Van Allsburg

Congratulations!

_____

name

has completed all the exercises in
this workbook and is ready
for kindergarten.

_____

date